Cabin Crew Interview ANSWERS Made Easy

Fifth Edition by Caitlyn Rogers,

Published by:
SpineBound Books
United Kingdom

ISBN: 978-1-908300-08-9

Printed in the United Kingdom
10 9 8 7 6 5 4 3 2 1

Library of Congress Cataloging-in-Publication Data
A CIP catalogue record for this book can be obtained from the British Library

Cover Photography Credits

Photographer:	Andrey Yakovlev
Art Director:	Tat'yana Safronova
Model:	Natal'ya Yarunicheva
Style, Makeup:	Lili Aleeva
Hair Style:	Ovo Arakelyan

With special thanks to AeroFlot Airlines

SPINEBOUND BOOKS

www.SpineBound.co.uk

Disclaimer

FROM THE PUBLISHER

This book is designed to provide information and guidance on attending a cabin crew assessment. It is sold with the understanding that the publisher and author are not engaged in rendering legal or other professional services. Such topics, as discussed herein are, for example, or illustrative purposes only. If expert assistance is required, the services of a competent professional should be sought where you can explore the unique aspects of your situation and can receive specific advice tailored to your circumstances.

It is not the purpose of this guide to reprint all the information that is otherwise available to candidates but instead to complement, amplify and supplement other texts. You are urged to read all the available material, learn as much as possible about the role and interview techniques and tailor the information to your individual needs.

Every effort has been made to make this guide as complete and accurate as possible. However, this guide contains information that is current only up to the printing date. Interview processes are frequently updated and are often subject to differing interpretations. Therefore, there are no absolutes and this text should be used only as a general guide and not as the ultimate source of information.

All information in this book is offered as an opinion of the author and should be taken as such and used with discretion by the reader. You are solely responsible for your use of this book. Neither the publisher nor the author explicitly or implicitly promises that readers will find employment because of anything written or implied here.

The purpose of this guide is to educate and inform. The author and SpineBound Books shall have neither liability nor responsibility to you or anyone else because of any information contained in or left out of this book.

The views and opinions expressed within this guide are those of the author and do not represent the views of any airlines or organisations named within. Any airlines mentioned are for the purpose of demonstration only. This book is neither associated, approved, affiliated with, nor endorsed by any airline.

My Dedication

TO YOU

This book is dedicated to all my readers who refuse to give up on their dream.

Thank you and good luck

Get updates
ONLINE

Updates, special offers and newsletters will be made available at:

www.CabinCrew.guide

So be sure to stop by.

www.CabinCrew.Guide

Where dreams are made

PART 1
THE INSIDE SCOOP

PART 2
MAKE YOURSELF UNFORGETTABLE

PART 3
QUESTIONS AND ANSWERS

THE

INSIDE SCOOP

PART I

Contents
Of this Session

A gruelling
PROCESS...

Interviews have always been nerve wracking experiences, however, the new style of behavioural questioning has made the final cabin crew interview a particularly gruelling process. Questions are fired in a way that actually keeps you from knowing what to say in response, and yet the recruiters are looking for quick and well-prepared answers.

Under this pressure, candidates are often thrown off guard and, information that would never otherwise be revealed, is openly volunteered as they struggle to come up with appropriate answers on demand. And, if this wasn't enough, recruiters are able to use a variety of tactics to trick candidates into volunteering sensitive information that would be illegal to ask in an interview. It is this kind of information that recruiters use to unfairly eliminate you and large numbers of other unsuspecting candidates.

. . . Designed
TO ELIMINATE

We'd all like to think that recruitment personnel are giving their undivided attention to each resume they receive, and we'd also like to think that every candidate would receive a fair and equal opportunity to interview for the position. The unfortunate truth is, each airline receives thousands of applications every month. This not only puts a great deal of pressure on recruitment teams to reduce the load, but also makes it very difficult for any one candidate to stand out. After seeing hundreds of hopefuls, it is only natural that faces and resumes begin to blur, with each sounding and looking much the same as the next.

To address this overload, airlines have become highly selective and candidates are put through a gruelling screening process, whereby hidden assessments and trick questions provide recruitment personnel an opportunity to secretly eliminate large numbers of unsuspecting candidates as early as possible. In essence, the process is no longer one that is designed to screen for the right candidate or the best fit, but rather to filter and eliminate.

What was once a merely challenging process has morphed into a barrage of trick questions, underhand tactics, psychological traps, and secret criteria. Each designed to whittle down the numbers as quickly as possible, leaving those candidates who are unprepared and uninformed feeling bewildered and confused by the whole process.

Run-of-the-mill

CLICHES WILL NOT CUT IT

Generic answers such as: I'm a workaholic, a perfectionist and I always try to please everyone are no longer going to cut it and neither is memorising lists of answers. In fact, memorising answers and trying to prepare for every possible scenario will work against you. Not only do you run the risk of sounding like a robot, with a boring and flat delivery, you are also more likely to be caught off guard by the aggressive and fast-paced style of questioning.

Within this guide, you will be shown how to create powerful answers that are flexible and can be applied to any scenario. You will learn why airlines use these trick questions, what the recruiter is secretly screening for and how to spot one so that you can avoid being culled by their deceptive tactics. No longer will you be cursed with run-of-the-mill and uninspiring answers that will have you sounding like everyone else, but can enter the process sounding like a top candidate.

So get ready, as you are about to learn about the interview process from an entirely different viewpoint.

WHAT TO
EXPECT

What to expect

Congratulations if you have made it through to the final interview. Having assessed your involvement and performance during the group sessions, the recruiters have clearly observed qualities in your character that they admire, and would now like to explore your motives further. So revel in the success you have achieved to this point, and be ready to close out this process.

During the final interview, the recruiters will seek to explore your motives for applying to the airline and your desire for pursuing a career as cabin crew. Moreover, they will seek to gather information about your work history, character and work ethic to determine whether you will fit the job and airline.

To ease you into the interview process, and make you feel more relaxed, the recruiters will typically open the session with questions about you and your background. They will then seek to explore your motivation for applying to the airline and making a career change. Questions such as "Why do you want to work for us?" and "Why do you want to be cabin crew?" are common at this stage.

With the interview thoroughly under way, the recruiters will want to determine whether you possess the skills and experience necessary for the position. Here you can expect more probing situational and behavioural questions, such as "When have you handled a customer complaint?" and "Describe a time when you failed to communicate effectively".

Although there appears to be no typical duration for panel interviews, you can expect a baseline time of at least 20 minutes, to upwards of 1 hour or more. In either case, the duration has no bearing on your ultimate success; so do not overly concern yourself with this aspect. An interview lasting just 20 minutes doesn't indicate a failure, just as an interview in excess of 1 hour does not indicate success.

Meet the

RECRUITMENT TEAM

Typically, there will be two or three official recruitment officers present during the final interview. These officers may be HR personnel, or they may be working senior crewmembers. Either way, you can be sure that they are experienced recruitment professionals.

To successfully interact with these recruitment personnel, it is important to understand their styles and be prepared to deal with them accordingly. Within a cabin crew interview setting, you will typically encounter two dominant styles of interviewer. I call these: The interrogation experts and the guardian angels.

The interrogation expert

Interrogation experts believe that candidates will only show their true personalities while under intense pressure. As a result, they adopt a direct and intimidating style of questioning and will cross-examine every answer you provide. During this onslaught of questioning, they will be observing your ability to remain calm and think on your feet. So, approach their questions in a calm and confident manner and be direct and succinct in your response.

The guardian angel

Guardian angels will attempt to relieve the pressure of the atmosphere by engaging in friendly conversation. While their relaxed and friendly style can be a welcome relief, unsuspecting candidates may become overly casual and reveal more than is appropriate. Caution is therefore advised to avoid being culled by these friendly tactics. You certainly don't to want to appear rigid, but you do need to be mindful of who you are talking to and remain professional.

What assessors
ARE REALLY LOOKING FOR

Recruiters understand that you will not be able to answer every question perfectly, and they also understand that you may not know the answer to each question that is asked. What they do expect and what they are interested in is how you respond to certain lines of questioning and how you conduct yourself. As such, their line of questioning will be designed to reveal your ability to:

- Listen actively
- Express yourself articulately, confidently and professionally
- Answer questions logically and concisely
- Remain calm under pressure

Some of the questions are designed specifically to throw you off guard, to see how you react to the pressure. With these sorts of questions, the interviewers are not necessarily looking for a perfect answer, but they are looking for a quick and well-prepared response.

They will also use several tactics to elicit a negative reaction or encourage you to reveal more than you should. This may be through the use of the silent treatment (as discussed in part 1), or through a line of questioning that is designed to keep you from knowing the correct answer. They will use trick questions, behavioural questions and even trick questions in the guise of a positive question, all in an attempt to rattle you and make you fall apart during the process.

Ultimately, it is important to remember that the recruiters are looking to hire positive people, so it is important to remain calm and composed throughout the interview and never show that you have been flustered.

Behavioural

QUESTIONS

Cabin crew interview questions are fairly unique, in that the majority of the questioning tends to focus almost exclusively on personal qualities and behavioural questions. As a result, there are no right or wrong answers, just more appropriate answers and better forms of expression.

This style of interview is often referred to as behavioural or situational, and the reason for this style of interview is because how you have applied certain skills and behaved in the past is often a clear indication of how you will behave in the future. In essence, the interviewers are looking to predict your future performance and determine if you have the qualities required to perform the duties of the role.

Behavioural interviews are nerve wracking experiences, and they are designed that way on purpose.

The key to preparing for this type of interview is to study the job description and person specification. Only then will you truly identify and understand what the interviewers want to hear and what they are screening for. With this knowledge, you can tailor your answers to match and demonstrate those competencies.

Because you will not know what questions will be asked, it is important to enter the process with 3-5 short stories that highlight the most important core competencies. At the bare minimum, try to have an example which demonstrates a team working , customer service, communication and a challenging experience. When the interviewer asks a question that relates to your story, you will have an example ready to launch.

THE TRICKS THE TRAPS AND THE UNDERHAND TACTICS

The telephone

SCREENING TRAP

In a quest to save time and money, some airlines are now adopting telephone-screening techniques. The telephone screening allows selectors to eliminate unsuitable candidates without going to the expense of inviting them to attend an interview.

As is the case with the interview, this initial telephone screening is laden with tricks and traps. The most cunning of these traps is the time the call takes place. Recruiters will often ring at inopportune times, such as first thing in the morning, on a weekend or during teatime. The reason they do this is because they are hoping to catch the candidate in their natural, and hectic environment. Are there children screaming in the background? Do you answer the telephone in a friendly tone or an unwelcoming one? And if you are caught at a bad time, how do you handle it?

They may also use the friendly recruiter routine to encourage dialogue, the abrupt end and the awkward silence. Each of which can be extra tricky when you cannot observe their body language or facial expression.

As you cannot predict when the call will come, you should be prepared as soon as you submit a resume or application form. At any time you get an incoming call from an unknown number, take yourself into a quiet room, and be sure to answer in a polite and friendly manner.

If you are caught at an inopportune time, politely ask the caller to hold for a brief moment while you move to a quiet location. Alternatively, if the timing is really bad, you can respectfully request an alternative date and time by saying "I do apologise, but is there a time I can reach you later? I'm very interested in the position and want to give you my undivided attention, but I'm afraid that now isn't the best time."

Icebreaker
OR DEAL-BREAKER

The interviewers will have several tricks up their sleeves to extract information during the course of the interview, but it is during the pre-interview 'ice breaking' session that you must be extra cautious.

During the first few moments of an interview it is only natural that most candidates will be feeing nervous, and it is under the rush of adrenaline that candidates are most likely to reveal too much information. It is also during these first few moments that candidates get caught off guard because they expect to be softly broken into the interview before the interrogation actually begins. Interviewers use this assumption to their advantage.

Personnel are trained to use trick questions, in the form of icebreakers, to get candidates to inadvertently volunteer sensitive and personal information about their circumstances and background. They will use friendly manipulation and small talk to lull candidates into a false sense of security. Under these conditions, they are able to extract information very easily from unsuspecting candidates.

So, whatever happens and however relaxed the interviewers attempt to make you feel, remember that you are being assessed and you need to keep your whit's about you.

The friendly
INTERVIEWER ROUTINE

The friendly interviewer routine is one that catches even the most seasoned candidates off guard. You enter the interview room and are surprised to discover that you are greeted by a warm and friendly welcome. The interviewer chats openly about all sorts of things, almost as if you are just catching up with an old friend. They make you feel at ease and, as you feel like you are starting to make a connection with this friendly individual, you suddenly find yourself letting your guard down.

Maybe you feel that you've created some sort of friendship. Maybe this interviewer is looking to help you get a job. Wrong! Interviewers are trained to be enthusiastic and friendly representatives of the airline, and it is this friendly approach that lulls candidates into a false sense of security. Under these relaxed conditions the interviewer is able to get a better sense of who you really are, and before you know it you begin revealing sensitive information about your home life, financial problems, health, former employer and challenges you are facing. By the time you realise that you've said too much, it's already too late.

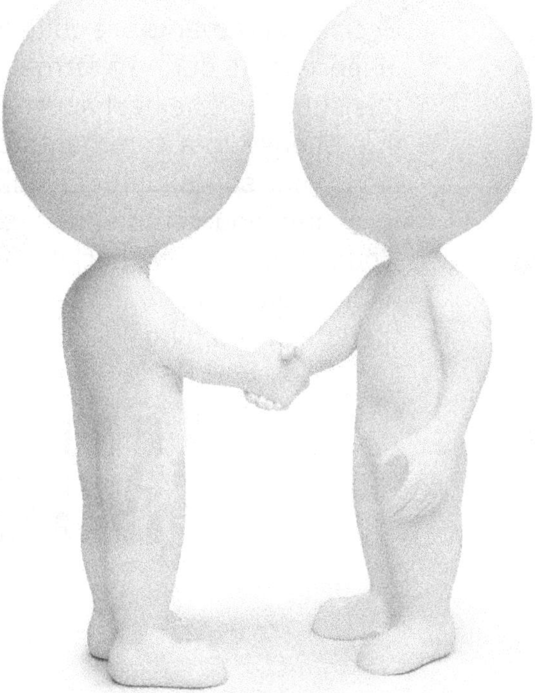

Whenever you meet the interviewer for the first time, it is important not to be taken in by this friendly approach. You certainly don't to want to appear rigid, by any means, but you do need to be mindful of who you are talking to and remain professional.

The lull of reciprocation

Following on from the friendly interviewer routine is the lull of reciprocation tactic. This tactic is probably one of the sneakiest because it is very easy to be taken in if you are unprepared. Here's how it works:

You enter the interviewer's office and the officer casually begins to open dialogue with some small talk about their children, or complains about their knee as they struggle to take their seat. Harmless? Unfortunately not! The purpose of this dialogue is to encourage a reciprocal response. For those candidates who are parents themselves, it is only natural that they too will begin to talk about your own children in response to such a comment. Or if a candidate is facing health struggles of their own, they may feel compelled to share out of empathy or politeness. 3178

These are just two examples, but there could be many more related to age, marital status, or your employment history. The list could go on.

Reciprocal remarks are quite acceptable in a social setting, but are completely inappropriate during a formal interview. So if you ever find yourself faced with this situation, the best approach is to respond with a question. For instance, in response to a comment about their children, you could ask, 1405 "How old is your son/daughter?" Likewise, in response to any statements relating to health, you could simply state "oh dear, I'm sorry to hear of your knee trouble. How did you hurt it?" These responses maintain a friendly connection, without giving anything away. In most cases, this will be sufficient to move the interview along.

MISERY LOVES COMPANY

The guise

OF A POSITIVE QUESTION

Lets say that partly through the interview when the recruiter asks how soon you can start. This is a simple question and one that has positive connotations. Unfortunately, this is an example of a trick question, which has been disguised as a positive one. When candidates hear this question, the natural response is one of excitement as they feel they are being offered the job. Without much thought, they begin to express a willingness to get started straight away.

The problem with this response is that if you are in employment your answer indicates that you are not willing to provide appropriate notice, and therefore will not be fulfilling obligations to your current employer. This surely does not work in your favour.

The best answer in response to this question is to affirm, "I have the energy and enthusiasm to start straight away. All I need is two week's notice for my current employer".

The Awkward
SILENCE

One of the most common interview traps you will encounter is the silent treatment. With this trick, the interviewer will respond to your answer with a blank stare and a deadening silence. This trick is so incredibly effective because most candidates are so intimidated by silence that they will often rush to fill the void.

Rather than see the silence as just a pause for thought, many candidates will view the silence as an indication that they have just goofed up in some way. It is in their haste to justify and recover their answer that they then volunteer irrelevant or damaging information, often appearing flustered and knocking themselves out of contention.

The point of using silence is to see how you respond to stress, therefore, whenever you are confronted with silence, the best strategy is to remain silent yourself. If the silence persists after 5-10 seconds, you can proceed to ask "is there anything I can add to clarify this point?" or "Did I answer the question fully enough?" These questions will demonstrate that you are not intimidated by silence or stress and will put the responsibility clearly back onto the interviewer. If there is something troubling him or her, this will encourage disclosure and an appropriate opportunity for you to reiterate.

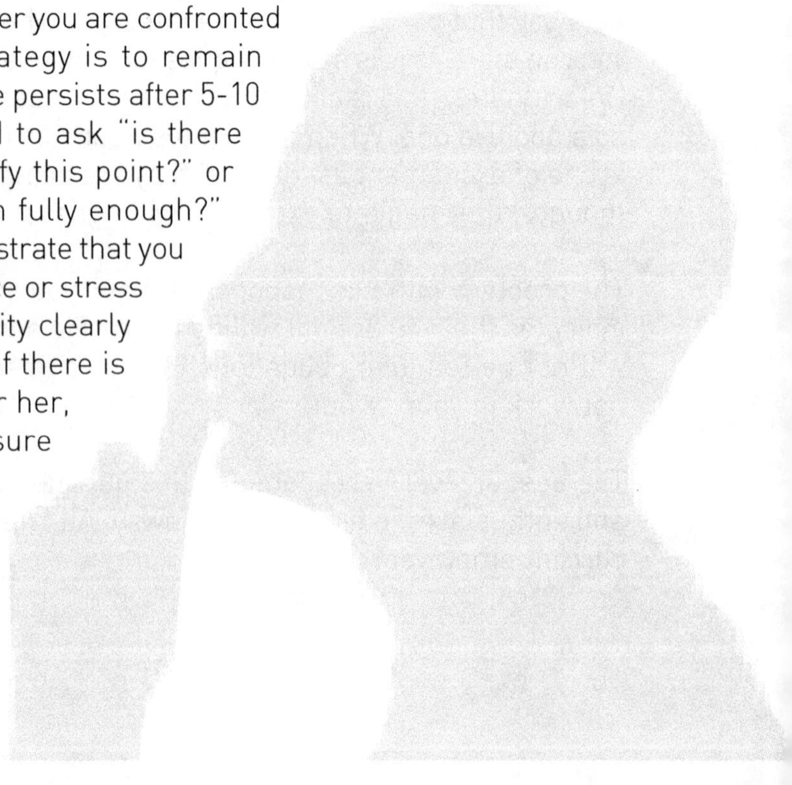

Probing with
FOLLOW-UP QUESTIONS

Follow up questions are either used to verity the viability of your answer, or to tempt negative information into the open. So it is important to have examples ready to back up any statements made.

Prepare to be asked:

- What did you learn from the experience?
- What specifically did you say?
- How did you feel?
- Would you do anything differently?
- How did they react?
- What other options did you consider?
- Why did you decide to take the action that you did?
- You mentioned ... Tell me more about that.
- How did you retain your composure?
- Can you give me an example of that?
- Can you be more specific about...?

The constant

INTERRUPTION

In an attempt to throw you off, the recruiter may even interrupt your responses with supplementary probing questions.

Take a look at the following example.

When have you disagreed with a colleague?

Candidate
"Working in a creative environment with other highly skilled professionals, it was natural that we had the occasional clash of ideas."

Recruiter
"Please can you elaborate further?"

Candidate
"We would sometimes have a clash of ideas based around our individual preference towards certain products, styles, magazines or equipment. Although, any disagreements we did have were relatively minor and insignificant."

Recruiter
"What would you consider minor and insignificant?"

Candidate
"Our debates were never confrontational, and they never interfered with our work in any way. In fact, some disagreements were quite educational."

Recruiter
"Educational?"

Candidate
"Yes, some very interesting views emerged from these debates which sometimes resulted in people, including myself, having a slight change in perspective."

Recruiter
"Can you tell me about a change you had in perspective following such a debate?"
...

It is important to answer the questions without demonstrating any frustration or resentment, Once you have answered the quesiton, smile and get straight back on point.

The abrupt end

The abrupt end is just how it sounds. All of the sudden, as if from out of nowhere, the interviewer declares an end to the interview. They show you to the door and thank you for your time. What should you make of this?

This sort of abrupt end is very similar to the silent treatment trick, in the sense that the interviewer is seeking your reaction to the stress of uncertainty. At this point, the formal interview really is over, however, your assessment is not. Your reaction will be observed very closely as you depart from the room and exit the premises. Do you remain composed or do you storm out of the building in defiance? Do you acknowledge the receptionist on your departure or simply ignore them?

As soon as you realise that the interview has reached its conclusion, regardless of what has happened and how you are feeling, it is important to depart gracefully for that final lasting impression.

Gather your belongings and, as you rise from your seat, straighten your clothing. Upon standing, thank the interviewer for his or her time and offer a final handshake. Make your way towards the door, stop and turn, and say your final thank you before making your exit. As you approach the front desk, acknowledge the receptionist with a sincere thank you and continue on your way. Only when you are clear of the area can you let out the scream of defiance, not before.

Does this abrupt end mean that you have been unsuccessful? Absolutely not! In fact, if handled well it could mark your success.

MAKE YOURSELF

UNFORGETTABLE

PART 2

Contents
Of this Session

Create a
MEMORABLE IMPRESSION

When faced with hundreds, and possibly thousands, of candidates, merely creating a good impression just isn't enough. You need to be memorable. The trouble is, very few people know how to truly differentiate themselves from the competition. Most candidates enter the interview in their own little bubble, thinking that they only need to dress well and sell their skills and experience. Unfortunately, this is only a small part of it.

Creating a memorable impression goes far beyond what you wear and how you carry yourself, and even beyond the skills and experience you posses. In fact, it is so rare that only 2% of candidates ever make it through to being hired.

The secret to creating a memorable impression will surprise you in its simplicity, and yet many candidates are unaware that such an advantage even exists, let alone know how to evoke it. They often enter the process only prepared for the hard sell, if they are prepared at all, and end up merely blending in with the rest of the crowd.

Recruiters see this same thing time and time again, so any candidate who is prepared to put in just that little bit of extra effort will naturally stand out, and it is these candidates who, ultimately, get hired.

So what is this mysterious phenomenon and how can you use it to your advantage?

The Art

OF THE CONNECTION

This technique is actually not mysterious at all. In fact, it is not even a secret. The technique involves creating a connection or, most commonly referred to as, establishing a rapport. Rapport is such a powerful tool, as it is the quickest way to achieve a sensation of familiarity and trust between you and the recruiter. It is so powerful, in fact, that it can even sway the hiring decision in your favour.

Why does this technique work so well? Have you ever met someone for the first time and yet you felt a strong connection, just as if you'd known him or her forever? This is rapport in action. If you can establish this level of rapport with the recruiter or undercover officers, you can be sure they will remember you favourably.

The quickest and easiest way to achieve a connection this strong is through the act of mirroring.

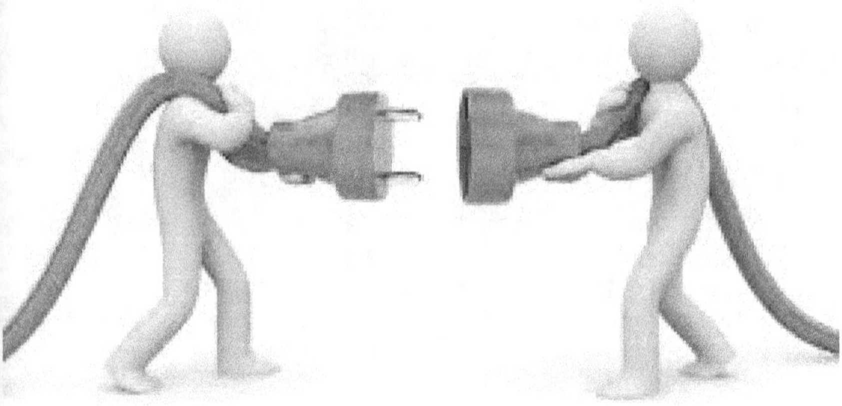

Mirror, Mirror

Mirroring is a process whereby you match your communication style, posture and mannerisms to those of another person. It is something you do naturally when you are deep in rapport with another person and is created by a deep feeling of unity. Using it consciously can evoke the sensation that the two of you are very much in sync just as readily as if it had occurred at a subconscious level, only you can be in control and use it to your own advantage.

As a note of caution, mirroring is something that must be done subtly to be effective. As such, it is important not to match every movement and not to react instantly to every change, else your motives will become obvious and the effectiveness of the technique will be lost.

For seamless results, take note of the following guidelines.

Body Language

As you are speaking with the recruiter, make a mental note of how they are sitting or standing, and what they are doing with their hands. Then, subtly mirror their position and gestures. If they are leaning forward, you might lean forward also. If they have their hands clasped on the table, you might do the same.

The best time to mirror a position is when you engage in dialogue. For example: The recruiter leans forward as he or she begins to ask you a question. As you engage in your follow up response, a change in position would appear natural and go completely unnoticed.

Be cautious not to mirror any closed signals, such as crossing your arms, as this will only accomplish a negative connection.

Communication Style

Mirroring a communication style can be done through using similar words or phrases, matching the sensory style, or mimicking the pitch, tempo and volume of their voice.

Words and Phrases

You can make a fantastic psychological impact simply by injecting the recruiter's own terminology and sequence of words into your answers. For example, if the interviewer points out that they are looking for and value a candidate who is 'team spirited', inject the same phrase into your answer. Simply stating that "I work well in a team", or "I am a team player", while implying the same values, will not create the same strong psychological impact as using the interviewers own words.

Pitch, Tempo and Volume

Matching your pitch, tempo and volume to the recruiters speaking style will make you appear in tune to what they are saying. This will speed up the rapport process and greatly improve your chances of creating a favourable impression. Keep pace with the interviewer and assess their basic conversational style. If they have a fast pace, assume the same characteristics. If they are analytical and introspective, slow down your responses to their speed.

Sensory Style

While we all use a mix of the sensory styles: Visual, kinaesthetic and auditory, we tend to have a dominant style that we gravitate towards. If, during the course of the interview, it becomes obvious that the recruiter has a preference towards a particular sensory style, you can adjust your style accordingly to establish a deeper connection.

Visual people use words that reflect their visual style, such as: 'I see what you mean', 'It looks to me like...', 'I imagine that...'

Auditory people use hearing words, such as: 'I hear what you are saying', 'We'll discuss this further', 'I hear you loud and clear'

Kinaesthetic people use action words, such as: 'It feels as if...', 'It slipped my mind', 'I have a solid grasp...'

Next time you are in a public place, observe how people who appear to be closely connected do these same things. You could even try this out for yourself next time you are out for lunch with a close friend or family member. In fact, because this technique can appear uncomfortable and awkward the first time you try it, practicing will, in time, make it almost natural and automatic, and you may even find that your relationships begin to blossom more than usual.

Leading

Leading is an influencing technique that can be used to judge the level of connection. For example: If you feel you have achieved rapport with the recruiter, you could change position or make a gesture to see If the recruiter follows your lead. If this does occur, you can be sure that you have established a strong connection. It the test reveals that the connection is not as strong as you thought, simply go back to mirroring to re-establish and strengthen the connection.

Disconnection

It is important to be perceptive to signs that the recruiter has become disconnected so that you can be proactive in re-establishing the connection.

Before attempting to reconnect, however, it is important to establish the accuracy of your perceptions because you may have simply misread the signal or it could be a by-product of a paranoid imagination. Similarly, the perceived signal may be a momentary motion that has no substance or it may be unrelated to you entirely.

To reliably determine the accuracy of your observation, you first need to scan for clusters of signals that are supportive of your perception. If you observe two or more congruent signals, this is a definite cluster. Next, you can test our connection by attempting to 'lead' (see above). If the recruiter doesn't follow, this is also a sure sign that a disconnection has taken place.

When to use it

During the group stages, you will not have an opportunity to forge any kind of connection with the official recruiters, however, you will be up close and very personal with the undercover team and it is here that you will be focusing much of your attention during these early stages.

The trouble is, how do you know who is undercover and who is a candidate? Unfortunately ,you don't. As such, the only possible way to accomplish this task is to make this same effort with every candidate you meet. While this may seem like an arduous and inefficient task, your efforts will pay off many times over, as you will gain an advantage like no other. In the worst instance, you will come away with a few new friends.

During the latter stages of the final interview, you can refocus your efforts on the official recruiters. This is where the technique will really come into its own and you can use it to its full advantage.

The one type

WHO ALWAYS GETS THE JOB OFFER

As you can now see, there is always one type who gets the job offer, but it isn't the best looking one as myths and legend would have you believe. The simple truth is that recruiters hire those individuals that they personally like and feel a connection with.

The biggest mistake most candidates make is that they enter the interview focused only on themselves and miss any opportunity to make a connection. A candidate who makes an effort will not only come across as more genuine and sincere, they will also instantly differentiate themselves from the competition, so it is certainly worthwhile putting the extra effort into perfecting this technique.

Just like

OLD FRIENDS

Another trick, which can be used as an adjunct to the previous technique, is to think of the recruiter as a good friend. Now I am not suggesting you take this literally, or you risk appearing too informal and familiar, what I am suggesting is that you enter the interview in a natural and conversational frame of mind.

The point of this technique is to help you relax, but also to assist the interviewer in breaking the ice. Simply initiating some friendly dialogue as you first meet the recruiter will help you to create an aura of a warm and approachable person, but also one who is relaxed and confident. Such a personable approach can help the interviewer feel more comfortable in your presence and will certainly get the interview off to a great start.

Naturally you will want to use common sense here to avoid stepping over the invisible line, however, it is important to remember that most candidates will only be thinking about themselves. The interviewer will appreciate your effort to connect.

The enthusiastic
APPROACH

If there is just one more thing that can set one candidate apart from the rest, it is the expression of a sincere passion and enthusiasm for the job, airline and the opportunity. Sadly, many people believe that showing enthusiasm will be mistaken for desperation and, as such, suppress their enthusiasm in favour of the laid back and relaxed approach. The truth is, the laid back approach is often mistaken for indifference or disinterest, and this can severely hinder your chances of success.

Another misconception is that being enthusiastic means that you need to be loaded with energy and bouncing off the walls. This is bordering on excitement, rather than enthusiasm, and is not ideal either. As discussed previously, the idea is to match the tempo of the person you are speaking to, and injecting too much energy can make it difficult for others to relate and connect with you, not to mention exhausting. You can certainly be calm and still be enthusiastic.

So what exactly is enthusiasm and how can you use it appropriately?

Use it appropriately

There are several ways that you can display your enthusiasm. This could be through an eagerness and willingness to learn, your facial expression and smile, an expression of pride in your work, actively listening and asking questions, taking notes and even through your knowledge and research about the opportunity and the airline.

You can also be upfront about your enthusiasm by stating it directly. For instance, when asked "Why do you want to be cabin crew?", speak from the heart as you tell them your personal story and the steps you have been taking to achieve your dream. If you have a sincere passion for meeting people from different cultures, express it. If you have a genuine love for assisting in the comfort of others, use it. If you have been participating in volunteer work to enhance your skills for the position, tell them. This is truly where you will stand head over heels above the run-of-the-mill answers that they hear 95% of the time.

Don't underestimate the power

It sounds simple, and even, superfluous, when compared to tangible skills and experiences, however, do not underestimate the power of honest and sincere enthusiasm. It is contagious and will energise those around you. More importantly, recruiters will pick up on your positive energy and will sense that you will approach the job with vigour.

Seven

HEAVENLY VIRTUES

1 Stay focused

If you fail to control your internal dialogue you will not only lose your composure, but you also risk misunderstanding the question. Remain completely focused on what the recruiter is saying and focus on giving the best possible answer. Concerns about how you look and the outcome should be postponed until after the interview.

2 Listen actively

Although you should never interrupt the recruiter, you shouldn't listen in total silence either. Instead, use verbal feedback cues to indicate that you are listening and that you understand. This will encourage the recruiter to continue. Some verbal feedback signals include: "I see", "Yes", "I understand", "Sure".

3 Inject personality

Injecting passion and personality into your answers will add life and sincerity. It will also keep the recruiters interested in what you are saying.

4 Be concise

If an answer is too long-winded, the recruiter will become complacent. Keeping your answers short and concise will retain their attention.

5 Vary your voice

Varying your tone, pitch, volume and pace will eliminate monotone and make it enjoyable for the recruiters to listen to. Slowing your pace slightly will also add clarity.

6 Be positive

A positive spirit will reflect well on your character and allow the recruiters to warm towards you. So, be enthusiastic about the interview and the job, and speak respectfully about your previous employers and positions.

7 Maintain eye contact

Regular, strong eye contact will give the impression of someone who is honest and confident. Where there is more than one recruitment officer, you should maintain eye contact with the person who asks you the question while occasionally engaging eye contact with the second recruiter.

Seven

DEADLY SINS

1 Controlling

Trying to lead or control the conversation will appear arrogant and disrespectful. Ask questions when appropriate opportunities arise, but allow the recruiter to do his or her job.

2 Interrupting

Interruptions are rude and disrespectful to the speaker. So, unless absolutely necessary, you should allow the recruiter to finish speaking before responding or asking for clarification.

3 Lying

If you lie, there will be a very good chance that you will be caught out when the recruiters probe into your answers with follow up questions. If this happens, you could end up looking rather silly and, worse still, any chance of being offered the job will be ruined.

4 Talking incessantly

It's easy to talk too much when nervous, however, it is important to remember that interviews are two-way exchanges. A moment of silence, while it might seem awkward to you, lets the recruiter know that you are done and allows them to move the interview along.

5 Being negative

Making negative remarks or exhibiting frustration over tasks, peers, other airlines or previous employers, no matter how harmless it may seem, will raise serious concerns about your attitude and ethics.

6 Overusing filler words

The useless and annoying verbal mannerisms "you know," "like," "in other words," "kind of," "ummm," and "anyways." should be avoided at all costs. Besides making you sound unprofessional, they also detract attention from your message.

7 Unprepared or unnecesary questions

To stand out as an informed and competent applicant, your questions should reflect that you have researched the airline and the position. Asking questions that have already been addressed within the airline's literature will make you appear unprepared and incompetent. Likewise, asking questions that are based on money and benefits will make you appear selfishly motivated and give a negative impression about your motives for the position and/or the airline.

Consider
YOUR COMMUNICATION

Because effective communication skills are essential for interview success, it is important to be mindful of how your communication is received. This means that you must consider not only the words you use, but also how your tonality and body language complement or contradict those words.

Consider the following communication guidelines:

Word choice

Words are important because they communicate and convey your message succinctly. So, even at a low 7% accountability, your word choice can mean the difference between a powerful, captivating and influential exchange, and a weak, disempowering and ineffective one.

! Action words

Action words are positive, powerful and directive, and should be used abundantly. Action words include: Communicated, conveyed, directed, listened, persuaded, arranged, handled and improved.

Filler words

Filler words are useless and annoying verbal mannerisms such as "you know," "huh," "erm," "kind of," "ummm," and "uh". Besides sounding unprofessional, they also distract attention from the message. Filler words should be avoided at all costs.

Undermining words

Words and phrases such as 'I think,' 'I hope,' 'maybe,' 'sort of,' 'perhaps,' 'I guess,' all undermine your message and credibility by creating the impression that you don't trust your own knowledge or opinion. Eliminating these phrases will drastically improve the quality of any message.

Jargon, slang and cliches

Specialist terminology and informal expressions can confuse an outside audience. Avoid these where possible, and stick to simple, clear and coherent language.

Vocal quality

Tonality plays a key role in sending the correct messages. So, if your aim is to project confidence, enthusiasm and expertise, it is important to exercise control and awareness of your tonality throughout your interactions.

Pitch

Pitch refers to the degree of highness and lowness in your voice. A variation in your pitch creates meaning, adds clarity and makes what you are saying more interesting. For instance: A rise in your pitch suggests you are asking a question, which indicates doubt, uncertainty and hesitation. A fall in pitch indicates a statement, which suggests certainty and assurance.

Tempo

Tempo refers to the speed of your voice. If you speak too slowly, you risk losing the interest and attention of your audience. If you speak too fast, others may find you difficult to follow. The key is to maintain a pace, which is fast enough to maintain interest, yet slow enough to be clear.

Volume

Speaking in a loud volume suggests aggression, while a quiet volume indicates shyness and makes it difficult to be heard. The key to determining the appropriate volume is to keep your voice loud enough to be heard, but soft enough to be clear. Modulation of volume can also be introduced to keep your speech interesting and add extra emphasis.

Articulation

Articulation refers to vocal clarity. Regardless of our pitch, tempo, volume and accent, you need to make a conscious effort to enunciate clearly.

Let your body
DO THE TALKING

The way you carry yourself, the gestures you use and your facial expressions communicate all sorts of messages. If you appear to lack confidence, seem evasive, or exhibit negative body language it is only natural that the interviewer will want to dig further to find out why your body is contradicting your words. So it is worth learning to control certain aspects so that you can convey the message of a well-balanced, confident individual.

The reason why your body language is so important is that it supports and reinforces what you say. In essence you appear to be exactly what you say you are.

Gestures

We use open gestures when we are feeling confident and relaxed, and are being honest and sincere, therefore, keep your arms unfolded, your legs uncrossed and your palms open. Sitting or standing with your arms crossed will be interpreted as a defensive posture and will give the impression that you are uncomfortable, bored, or have something to hide. Likewise, standing in your hands in your pockets suggests unease.

Touching your nose during the interview is commonly interpreted as an indication of dishonesty, so even if it itches, it is best to grin and bear it. Observe caution if you experience the tendency to rub your neck as this too can be misinterpreted as boredom or unease.

Gesturing can be useful for adding emphasis to what you are saying and, if the movements you employ are subtle and controlled, it is perfectly okay to use gestures to express yourself and endorse your words. For best results, keep any movements below shoulder level, but above the waistline.

Posture

Posture is fundamental to appearing alert, confident and motivated, and yet it is shocking to see how many candidates forget this one simple rule. Take a look around the room next time you attend a group interview and you will see candidates slouching and generally looking bored and inattentive while they wait to be assessed.

I understand that the wait can be long and tiresome, however, it is important that you do not let this happen to you. This is the period when you are being watched very closely and letting your posture relax too much will demonstrate disrespect and give the impression that you lack interest.

To portray the image of a confident and motivated person, adopt an upright and attentive posture that is open, yet relaxed. Keep your chin parallel to the floor, shoulders back and spine straight.

If seated, lean slightly forward with your hands loosely in your lap, or on the table. Place both feet flat on the floor, or cross your ankles. And always be sure to direct your body and your feet towards the interviewer and not at the door, as this will give the impression that you feel uncomfortable and are ready to flee.

If standing, keep your arms loosely at your side or behind your back and plant your feet about 8-10 inches apart. If standing for long periods, place one foot slightly in front of the other to allow you to smoothly and unnoticeably shift weight between your feet.

Your carriage

The way you carry yourself is a powerful indicator of how you feel. To be perceived as confident and professional, walk briskly with an erect posture. Keep your shoulders back, your arms loosely at your side, and chin parallel to the floor.

Facial expressions

Your facial expressions convey a wide range of attitudes, feelings and emotions, and these can have a significant impact on your ability to connect with others. Because of this, it is important to be aware of the story your face is telling and work to convey an attentive, sincere and interested expression.

A positive expression can certainly include a smile, but doesn't necessarily imply its inclusion. In fact, maintaining a constant smile is not only uncomfortable, but it is also completely unnecessary. Instead, an open expression that includes a gentle and understated smile, soft eyes and slightly elevated eyebrows will result in a soft and pleasant expression.

Large smiles should be reserved for introductions and the occasional injection during conversation.

Handshake

Your handshake says a lot about you. A firm handshake conveys confidence, assertiveness and professionalism while a weak, limp handshake suggests shyness and insecurity. A strong, crushing handshake indicates aggression and dominance, and should be avoided.

To perform a professional and confident handshake, follow these simple guidelines:

Before connecting for the handshake establish eye contact, smile and lean slightly forward. As you extend your right hand, keep your hand straight and thumb pointing upwards. When your hands connect engage a firm, but not crushing, grip. Pump one to three times, for a duration of 1-3 seconds, and break away.

The Eyes

DEFINITELY HAVE IT

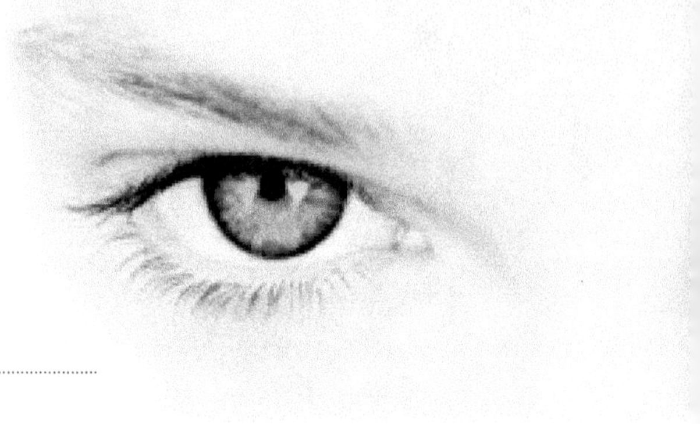

Your handshake says a lot about you. A firm handshake conveys confidence, assertiveness and professionalism while a weak, limp handshake suggests shyness and insecurity. A strong, crushing handshake indicates aggression and dominance, and should be avoided.

To perform a professional and confident handshake, follow these simple guidelines:

Before connecting for the handshake establish eye contact, smile and lean slightly forward. As you extend your right hand, keep your hand straight and thumb pointing upwards. When your hands connect engage a firm, but not crushing, grip. Pump one to three times, for a duration of 1-3 seconds, and break away.

Good eye contact is one of the most important factors of body language. Shifty eyes, or complete avoidance of contact can suggest dishonesty, boredom, rudeness, insecurity or shyness.

If you find eye contact anxiety provoking and uncomfortable, direct your gaze at their eyebrows, forehead, or bridge of the nose. This is not a permanent solution by any means, but it will certainly ease you into the process.

In an attempt to forge eye contact, be aware not to stare as this can indicate aggression and make others feel uncomfortable. To avoid this extreme, lighten your gaze and keep it friendly. This can be achieved by allowing your eyes to go slightly out of focus.

If you have notes, you can temporarily break eye contact as you refer to these, and if there is a second recruitment officer present, this will give you opportunity to break eye contact as you periodically direct your focus back and forth between the two.

Aim to maintain eye contact for 80-90% of the time.

CREATE

INSPIRING ANSWERS

TO ANY QUESTION

Answers

AS EASY AS **A.B.C**

When preparing your answers to traditional questions, keep the A.B.C formula in mind.

A Answer

Make your answer concise by answering the question directly

B Back it up

Back up your answer with solid facts. This will add a lot of weight to any statements made.

C Conclude

The conclusion allows you to expand on your skills and what you can offer the airline

Consider the following example:

What is your best attribute?

Answer:
"As you will have observed during the group assessments, I am a very welcoming and social individual who interacts well with others, and readily adapts to new people and environments."

Back it up:
"In fact, my previous supervisor also picked up on these attributes and often asked me to carry out the client shampoo because she knew I would make the clients feel welcome and relaxed"

Conclude:
"I am confident that this aspect of my character will enable me to perform the job to the same high standard that exists currently within the airline"

A.C.T
ON NEGATIVE QUESTIONS

Negative questions can be better approached using the A.C.T formula.

A Attack

By attacking the question head on, not only do you avoid being alienated by the question, it also allows you to swiftly move on and add clarity to your response.

C Clarify

This is your opportunity to add any clarity and facts that may support or justify your answer.

T Turn

Now turn the focus away from the initial negative question to focus on the positive outcome of the experience.

Consider the following example:

What is your greatest weakness?

Attack:
"I recognise that my leadership ability is a potential area of improvement"

Clarify:
"Which is why I am actively working on developing this area further through a part time training course at my local college"

Turn:
"Although I am still learning, I see constant improvement in my capabilities when being faced with leadership tasks and I am confident that I will continue to learn and grow with experience"

Winning answers

WITH THE **S.A.R.R** FORMULA

When preparing your examples to competency-based questions, the S.A.R.R formula can help you structure your response.

S Situation

Briefly describe the challenge, problem, or task

A Action

Describe what you did and how you did it

R Result

Describe the outcome and how your actions affected the outcome or the people involved

R Reflection

Elaborate on what you learned from the experience and whether you would do things differently in the future.

Consider the following example:

When have you used your initiative to solve a problem?

Situation:
"I was in the staff room during my lunch break, and I could hear a lot of noise coming from inside the salon. I went to investigate and two, very bored, little girls confronted me. I could sense that their excitement was causing a disruption and inconvenience"

Action:
"I immediately took the initiative and attempted to occupy them by offering to plait their hair while they made bracelets from some hair beads. Their eyes sparkled with excitement and I was able to keep them occupied for the remainder of their visit"

Result:
"We had lots of fun and, while the calm was restored, the stylist was able to complete the clients' treatment"

Reflection:
"I felt really pleased that with just a little extra effort, I had made such a big difference"

Avoid robotic

FLAT AND BORING ANSWERS

In preparing for the final interview, it may make sense to memorise some of your answers. Unfortunately, trying to memorise an answer for every scenario will only work against you. Not only do you run the risk of sounding like a robot, with a boring and flat delivery, but you also risk forgetting your answers and appearing flustered as you try to recall the information.

Rather than memorising your answers, make a list of key points and try to remember those instead. Key points are much easier to remember than lengthy sentences and will allow you to create a genuine and spontaneous answer based around that point.

Another technique, that is highly effective and advantageous, is to prepare through actual practice. Whether that is through a role play with a friend or family member, the use of a camcorder or through attending mock interviews with other airlines, practice will allow you to feel much more confident and natural when you do the real thing.

Demonstrate respect for the recruiter

It is important to be observant and sense when the interviewer has heard enough about a particular point. Many candidates go off on a tangent when they get into the swing of the interview, and neglect to notice that the interviewer wants to move on. To demonstrate your respect for the recruiter and his or her time, you could ask "Would you like me to elaborate on that further?" The interviewer will appreciate your effort.

Eek, I don't know the answer

You are not expected to know the answer to every question you are asked. In fact, the interviewer may throw you a curve ball on purpose in order to test you reaction and observe how you respond under the pressure.

Bluffing your way through an answer, for the sake of not wanting to admit that you don't know the answer, will not reflect favourably on you. The interviewer will be much more forgiving if you are honest and admit your lack of knowledge on a particular point.

If you lack relative experience in a particular area, you may consider elaborating on a similar and alternative aspect, or you can take the opportunity to remind them of the skills that you do have and explain how you would tackle the situation if it arose. For instance: "I can't remember ever being in that situation, however, I did face something slightly similar that I could tell you about?".

Use

ACTION PHRASES

Action phrases, made up of verbs, express action. They are positive, powerful and directive, and should be used abundantly throughout your interview.

Notice how using direct action verbs make the sentence powerful:

"As a hairdresser, I consulted with clients and provided advice"

The following page contains an extensive list of action verbs. Use them abundently throughout your

Action verbs

Achieved
Addressed
Advocated
Allocated
Analysed
Anticipated
Appraised
Approved
Arbitrated
Arranged
Assembled
Assessed
Attained
Authored
Balanced
Budgeted
Built
Calculated
Catalogued
Clarified
Classified
Coached
Collaborated
Collected
Communicated
Compiled
Conceptualised
Consolidated
Consulted
Contracted
Conveyed
Convinced
Coordinated
Corresponded
Counselled
Created
Critiqued
Customised
Delegated
Demonstrated
Designed
Developed
Directed
Enlisted
Established
Evaluated
Examined
Executed
Expedited
Explained
Expressed
Fabricated
Facilitated
Forecasted
Formulated
Founded
Generated
Guided
Handled
Identified
Illustrated
Implemented
Improved
Incorporated
Increased
Influenced
Informed
Initiated
Inspected
Instituted
Integrated
Interpreted
Interviewed
Introduced
Invented
Investigated
Lectured
Led
Listened
Litigated
Maintained
Marketed
Mediated
Moderated
Motivated
Negotiated
Operated
Organised
Originated
Overhauled
Oversaw
Participated
Performed
Persuaded
Pioneered
Planned
Presented
Produced
Projected
Promoted
Publicised
Recommended
Recruited
Reduced
Referred
Repaired
Reported
Represented
Researched
Resolved
Review
Reviewed
Revitalised
Scheduled
Shaped
Solved
Spearheaded
Spoke
Strengthened
Suggested
Summarised
Supervised
Systematised
Taught
Trained
Translated
Upgrades
Wrote

Stand out

AS AN INFORMED CANDIDATE

Taking the time to research an airline you want to work for will enable you to ask intelligent questions, as well as answer any that are posed. Your informed knowledge will give a positive impression about you and your motivation to work for the airline, thus giving you a competitive edge over less informed candidates.

If you know nothing about the airline other than the colour of the uniform, the salary and their best destinations, you certainly won't create a positive impression.

There is no need to know the whole history of the airline, but you should at least know some basic information, such as:

- What is their route network?
- Are there any future plans for expansion or growth?
- Where is their base airport located?
- Who are the airline's major competitors?
- What do you like about this particular airline?
- How long have they been operating?
- Has the airline won any awards? If so, which ones?

SURVIVAL 101

Resolve

COMMON CONCERNS

Challenge: Blushing

Go green
A purposeful green-pigmented concealer or foundation will minimise the impact of redness.

Seek medical advice
Blushing which is caused by a medical condition should be treated by a medical professional. Prescription medication may be prescribed.

Challenge: Cottonmouth

Cottonmouth is a natural and protective barrier, which is often caused by nerves. To minimise the effects, be sure to keep fully hydrated on the run up to the event. Fill up on water during breaks and periodically sip on water throughout the assessment.

You can stimulate saliva flow by adding a splash of lemon juice to your water bottle, sucking on sugar free candy or chewing sugarless gum. Gently biting your tongue can also activate the glands that stimulate saliva flow.

Avoid salty and sugary foods, alcohol (including alcohol based mouthwash), caffeinated beverages and tobacco products as these inhibit saliva flow and dry the mouth out further.

Challenge: Going blank

Even with all the preparation in the world, our mind can betray us and draw a blank at the most inopportune moment. If this happens, take a deep breath, remain composed and employ some of the following techniques:

Refer to your resume

Your resume provides an immediate memory jog in these instances, so refer to it as and when necessary. You may also want to jot down some key words or phrases inside a professional looking notebook beforehand.

Wait a moment

You don't have to always answer questions immediately. It is perfectly permissible to pause and collect your thoughts before proceeding with a response. In fact, taking the time to think through your response can make you appear deliberate and thoughtful. Answering without regard for your answer can make you look impulsive.

Be honest

If you don't have relative experience in a particular area, or simply don't know the answer, you need to be honest and say so. At this point, you could offer an alternative and or related answer.

Stall

If you feel you can get away with it, reflect the question back to allow yourself a little more thinking time.

Stay composed

Some recruiters will purposely throw in some curve ball questions to see how you react to pressure and think on your feet. In these cases, the interviewer is probably more interested in observing your reaction than they are about the answer you provide. So, stay calm and do your best to answer in a confident manner. In the worst case, simply be honest and admit you don't know the answer.

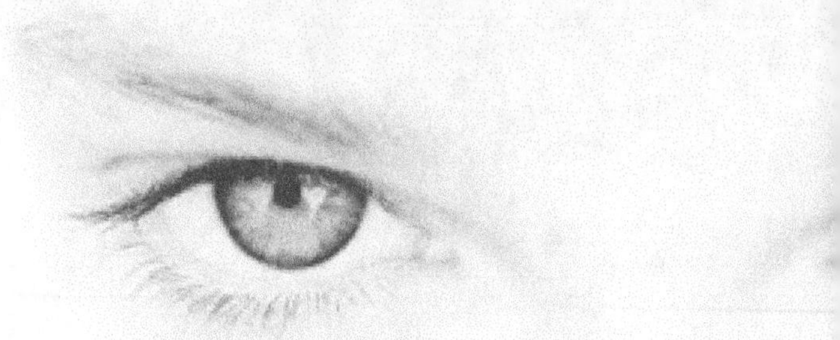

Challenge: Eye contact

Good eye contact is one of the most important factors of body language. Shifty eyes, or complete avoidance of contact can suggest dishonesty, rudeness or lack of confidence. If you find eye contact anxiety provoking and uncomfortable, the following techniques will certainly help.

Use a mirror
Practice your eye contact by using your own-mirrored image as a guinea pig. When you see yourself in the mirror every day, make a point of looking directly into your own eyes.

Fake it
Rather than look directly into the eyes, you can fake it by either directing your gaze at their eyebrows, forehead, or bridge of the nose. This is not a permanent solution by any means, but it will certainly ease you into the process.

Avoid staring
In an attempt to forge eye contact, you may begin to stare. This can indicate aggression and make others feel uncomfortable. To avoid this extreme, lighten your gaze to keep it friendly. This can be achieved by allowing your eyes to go slightly out of focus.

Use opportunities to break contact
If you have notes, you can temporarily break eye contact as you refer to these. Also, if there is a second recruitment officer present, this will give you another opportunity to break eye contact as you periodically direct your focus back and forth between the two.

Challenge: Fidgeting

Fidgeting, tapping and excessive gesturing with give the appearance of uncertainty, nervousness and unpreparedness. To effectively manage these movements, use the techniques outlined below.

Identify

If you are unsure of any habits you may have, ask a friend, partner or co-worker for their views. Alternatively, record yourself in a short mock interview and examine the footage. Mark down any ineffective mannerisms you can identify (playing with your pen, drumming your fingers, touching your face or hair, clearing your throat, or rubbing your nose) and then begin the process of consciously eliminating each of them.

Beware of props

Props can easily exaggerate any fidgeting, so if you have a pen, résumé or bag with you, avoid fiddling with them. Be equally mindful of jewellery, such as twirling earrings or a finger ring.

Mind your hands

If the movements you employ are subtle, it is perfectly okay to gesture your arms and hands to endorse your words. Subtle means, keeping the movements below shoulder height and above the waist. If you find your movements become excessive or distracting, simply intertwine your fingers and rest your hands on the table or clasped loosely in your lap.

Challenge: Perceived arrogance

Sometimes, a high level of confidence may be misconstrued as arrogance. If you feel you are sometimes wrongly labelled as arrogant, the following guidelines will help you maintain your confidence, while avoiding this assumption.

Be open
We all have weaknesses; to say otherwise will certainly make you appear arrogant. Be clear about what you do and don't know, and be prepared to listen and learn from others.

Be humble
Act with humility when you are recognised for a job well done. Acknowledge the effort of others by sharing and giving praise where appropriate, and be accountable when errors transpire.

Be approachable
To make yourself appear more approachable, use open and inviting body language, and adopt a warm, friendly expression. Inject some personality into your conversations, make good use of eye contact and remember to use people's names.

Be considerate
Genuinely acknowledge and compliment the hard work and efforts of others. Listen to and respect others opinions, and avoid interrupting when others are speaking.

! Challenge: Feeling uncertain

You don't always have to give an opinion when you speak. Supporting what someone else has said, asking a legitimate question, or commenting on an emerging theme are equally good ways to make your presence known without appearing as if you like the sound of your own voice.

Points to Consider

In most cases, the outcome of each task or topic is largely irrelevant. Assessors are more concerned with how well you perform in a team environment, how you communicate your ideas and interact with others, and what role you typically assume.

Thus, no matter how you feel, you should approach every task with a can do attitude and every topic in a calm and conversational tone.

Bloopers, blunders
AND FAUX PAS RECOVERY

We've all experienced a blunder at some time or another, from the ill-fated slip of the tongue, to the embarrassing body blooper. You name it, it's happened to the best of us.

In everyday circumstances, bloopers, blunders and faux pas can be brushed off and, hopefully, forgotten. But what do you do and how can you recover if this happens during the all-important interview event? Do you laugh it off? Apologise? Pretend it never happened? Blame someone else? Make a sharp and speedy exit, or maybe a combination of the above?

Just in case the unexpected should happen to you on your big day, I have devised some stealth tactics and faux pas recovery tips. Hopefully you will never have to use them, but at least you'll have a strategy if you need one.

Three effective approaches

Depending on the severity of the blunder, there are three ideal approaches you can take: The first is to simply ignore it and move into a smooth recovery. The second is to hold yourself accountable and apologise, and the third is to simply laugh it off.

So let's take a look at each of these strategies further.

The smooth recovery

In many instances, you may choose to simply ignore it and move straight into a smooth recovery. This can be a great option if the blunder was mildly insignificant or barely noticeable. The risk with this strategy is that many will use it as a means to forge ahead and hopefully disguise their embarrassment. Unfortunately this urge to keep talking can make things worse if you are rattled or fixated on the blooper. Instead of making a smooth recovery, you may find yourself babbling.

After a blooper, it is natural to feel embarrassed, but it is important that you don't become fixated or concerned about the blunder or the recruiter. You'll stand a much better chance of recovery if you stop, take a breath, smile and continue on.

The artful apology

For moments that cannot just be ignored or brushed aside, there is the artful apology. Apologising for a blunder or faux pas is a great way to demonstrate a sense of respect and character. Rather than trying to hide or make excuses, drawing attention to the mistake and then apologising will demonstrate that you are honest and not afraid to take responsibility. This is an admirable quality and should not be underestimated.

Most people are willing to forgive, and you'll be amazed at how disarming a simple apology can be. Moreover, once a genuine apology has been made, the case is closed and everyone can move on from it.

It is important to keep your apology simple, yet sincere. A statement such as "I do apologise, my nerves got away from me there" or "I'm sorry, that came out wrong. May I rephrase that answer?" is all that is required. Once the apology has been made, shift the attention away and continue as if nothing happened. Don't give in to the urge to offer a lengthy apology, and don't bring the incident up again.

Be willing to laugh at yourself

When all else fails, having a laugh at your own expense may be the only way to disarm your audience and smooth over the faux pas. It will certainly lighten any awkwardness that has emerged in the atmosphere and most people appreciate someone who is willing to laugh at their own mistakes. If nothing else, it will show that are you aren't easily rattled and at least have a sense of humour. Not bad qualities I'm sure you'll agree.

It's how you handle it that counts

Whatever blunder you encounter, remember that everyone makes mistakes, and it is how you handle the mistake that will be observed and remembered. So whether it is the unexpected burst of flatulence, the skirt caught in the panties or a flubbed answer, if you are able to keep your cool and make a smooth recovery, the recruiter will appreciate your ability to remain composed in a challenging situation.

QUESTIONS &

ANSWERS

PART 3

Contents
Of this Session

UNCOVERING
YOUR MOTIVES

Why do you want

TO BECOME CABIN CREW?

In order to stand out and differentiate yourself from the crowd, it is important to provide and honest and passionate response to this question. Think about it, why do you really want the job? Where did the desire come from? Was it a childhood dream, or was it sparked by another interest? A generic response involving the lure of travel and glamour will not be viewed positively. Be unique and be creative.

"As a child, I grew up very close to the airport and was fascinated by aircraft. I always felt a buzz of excitement when planes flew overhead and dreamt of someday working within the airline industry.

This is where my passion for flying initially began, but it wasn't until I carried out a career suitability test at college that I really started to consider cabin crew as a serious future prospect.

The test examined personal attributes, interests and skills, and the final result came back suggesting suitability for the occupation.

After this, I began to carry out further research into the job and, the more I researched, the more I realised that this is a job that is tailored to my personality, skills and experience. It is one I will feel committed to and I am confident that I will be good at."

Why do you
WANT TO WORK FOR THIS AIRLINE?

The interviewer is not interested in what the airline or position can do for you, they are more concerned with what you can bring to them. To make the greatest impact begin with a personal story, but close with a demonstration of your knowledge and fit for the airline. This will make you stand out as an informed and enthusiastic individual who has something to offer.

"My first passenger experience with Fly High Airlines was two years ago, on a flight from Dubai to Los Angeles. The service on board was so immaculate and welcoming, that I was instantly impressed. Following this experience I became a frequent flyer and, when I decided to apply for this position, I was in no doubt who I want to work for.

Once I started to research the airline further, I was pleased to discover that the airlines corporate culture holds true with my own values and beliefs. Specifically the open door policy and customer comfort initiatives. This discovery reinforced my desire further and confirmed my belief that I will indeed complement your existing team."

Have you applied to any other airlines?

"Although it is taking a bit of a risk, I haven't applied to other airlines because I am set on working for you. I wanted to see how my application went with you before I considered other options."

If another airline offered you a job, would you take it?

"Because I am set on making cabin crew my future career, if I did not get this job with you, then I would have to consider other airlines. However, Fly High Airlines are at the very top of my list and I would be naturally disappointed not to get the job with you."

Where do you picture yourself in five years?

"I very much hope that I shall be with Fly High Airlines in five years time. By which time, I will have made a significant contribution to the airline, will have become an experienced senior member of the cabin crew team, and will be working on new ways to advance my career further."

If offered the job, how long will you stay with us?

"I'm approaching this job with a long term view. I hope to make enough of a contribution the airline, that I can move up through the ranks to become an experienced senior member of the cabin crew team."

KNOWLEDGE ABOUT THE JOB AND THE AIRLINE

What do you know

ABOUT THIS JOB?

The recruiters want to know that you understand what the role involves and are not naive about the pressures and demands. Stand out by demonstrating your informed knowledge and research.

"I know that the service we see as passenger's form only a small portion of what actually goes on in the job. With safety being the primary concern, there are procedures and checks which must be constantly and consistently completed. Then, when things go wrong, cabin crew are there to take control. Moreover, it is a constant process of cleaning and preparation, paperwork and stock checks, tending to passenger comfort and being of service. Clearly the profession is a very demanding one, but it is also a very exciting and fulfilling one for the right person, which I do believe I am."

What qualities

ARE NECESSARY FOR CABIN CREW?

The recruiters want to know that you understand what the role involves and what qualities are necessary to perform its tasks. Conclude this answer by acknowledging your skills in relation to the position.

"Cabin crew play a vital role in giving a good impression of the airline as a whole. This means crew members need to have good communication and customer care skills, as well as a friendly and welcoming demeanour.

Because of the importance of safety, it is also important that they have the strength of character to cope with difficult people and situations, in a calm and objective manner.

These are all attributes I possess and have demonstrated throughout the 8 years of my career as a beauty consultant, and are the primary reasons I would complement your existing team."

Do you think

THE ROLE IS A GLAMOROUS ONE?

It is no secret that many candidates are drawn to the superficial lifestyle, travel and glamour associated with the industry. The recruiters are trying to determine your motives for seeking the position, but also want to understand that you are not naive about the real challenges and requirements of the position.

"Having thoroughly researched the position, I am aware that the glamour associated with the role is rather superficial. Sure there are benefits of travel, and the crew certainly do make themselves appear glamorous, but the constant travelling between time zones, the long and tiring shifts, unpredictable schedules and irregular working patterns place tough demands on crew and make the job anything but glamorous."

What do you think

ARE THE DISADVANTAGES OF THE JOB?

To deny the obvious drawbacks of the job will only make you sound naive and unprepared, so be up front about the disadvantages and demonstrate that you have considered these carefully.

"The obvious disadvantages are the flight delays and cancellations that crew experience. While passengers also experience these issues, crew experience those far more often. This makes for very long and tiring shifts, irregular working patterns and unpredictable schedules.

Moreover, the regular crossing between different time zones can take its toll leading to jet lag and fatigue.

Every position holds its own share of percieved disadvantages, so I understand them as a necessary part of the position and will do my best to take proactive measures to avoid or minimise any undue consequences. By applying for this position, I have accepted everything that comes with it."

What do you think are the advantages of this position?

"The randomness and variety of the different crew, passenger profiles, roster structure ,and the challenges of the position itself excite me greatly. They are unique elements that you just don't find in normal nine to five jobs. It's a position I will find rewarding in a number of ways."

What aspects of customer service are most important to our passengers?

"Passengers want to feel comfortable and looked after by the airline and crew. They want to be assured that crew will listen to and answer their questions, and will be friendly and polite in doing so. If crew are not approachable, passengers feel unwelcome and unsure."

What do you think contributes to passenger frustrations?

"Feeling tired from travelling can cause passengers to feel unusually frustrated. Add to this flight delays, long waiting times and space constrictions, and frustration naturally increases. If the passenger is then greeted by seemingly unwelcoming staff, their tension will certainly rise much further."

Why do you think some passengers vent their frustrations on cabin crew?

"In the first instance, cabin crew wear the airline's uniform. Thus, passengers consider them to be a representative of the airline. Moreover, the passengers spend more time with cabin crew than with any other member of the airline staff, so they simply become an easy target."

What do you know

ABOUT OUR AIRLINE?

This is where your research will pay off handsomely. Demonstrate your enthusiasm by sharing knowledge that will reveal the effort you have taken to learn more about the airline and its operations.

"Fly High Airlines began operating in 1980 with a single leased aircraft, serving just two destinations. The airline now serves 73 destinations in 48 countries worldwide and is rapidly expanding its route network, which is soon to include Bristol and Ohio.

As a testament to the airlines excellent standard of service, it has acquired over 250 international awards for customer service excellence, and is now one of the largest and popular airlines in the world.

On a personal note, I am a frequent flier with Fly High Airlines and have witnessed this standard of service first-hand, and it is these attributes that have drawn me towards this airline over the competition. "

How would you

RATE US AGAINST OUR COMPETITORS?

This question can be a tricky one to answer for those who are unprepared. If you read between the lines, you will see that interviewer is seeking to discover your understanding about the airline and its competition.

In answering this question, remain positive by focusing your answer on the advantages of the airline you are applying for and what they do well.

Example 1
"It's so difficult to be objective, and I really don't like to slight your competition."

Example 2
"My experiences with each of the airlines I have flown with have all been good, and I never had a problem or cause for complaint. An advantage of Fly High Airlines, however, is the attentiveness of the crew. They really take care of all their passengers and do everything to make the flight as pleasant as possible. I have always been made to feel welcome on board your flights.

Any airline can fly a customer from A to B, but it is the attentiveness of the crew that can mean the difference between a good experience and a pleasurable one. I can only hope I will be so lucky as to work for an airline who cares so deeply about its passengers as does Fly High Airlines."

Have you ever flown with us?

"Yes, I have had the fortunate opportunity to fly with Fly High Airlines on several occasions now. With the attentive crew, outstanding meal service and comfortable seating, I always feel as though I am flying first class. I am now a frequent flyer and very happy customer. I now hope to join your team in providing this fantastic service."

Do you think we have a good reputation?

"Absolutely! Through my own experience, I have encountered attentive and efficient crew, fantastic meals and comfortable seating. In researching the airline, it appears that others agree with these observations.

The variety of awards the airline has received over the years is a sure testament to its fantastic reputation."

What is the worst thing you have heard about us?

"The worst thing I have heard about Fly High Airlines is that competition for jobs is fierce because it is such a terrific airline. Everything else I have heard, have been overly positive."

Is there anything you think we do badly?

"In conducting my research into the airline, I haven't come across anything to suggest that you are doing anything badly. In fact, I have discovered quite the opposite.

Plus, I am sure you wouldn't enjoy your current success and be receiving so many awards for excellence if you were doing anything really wrong."

How do you feel about working for a small airline?

"I have always valued the feeling of a small company. They haven't become large and impersonal and I like the potential for being involved in the growth of the airline."

How do you feel about working for a large airline?

"I welcome the opportunity to work in a large, developed and well known airline such as this. The resources and potential for advancement are not available in smaller airlines. I'd be proud to apply my skills and abilities to the excellence that flourishes here."

ASCERTAINING YOUR SUITABILITY

Tell me

ABOUT YOURSELF

While this question is often used to break the ice, it is also asked to gain a true sense of who you are. Its open-ended and unstructured approach will reveal a great deal about you and what you feel is important.

The best approach is to provide a short paraphrased overview of what you do, why you are attending the interview and what you have to offer.

"As you can see from my résumé, I currently work as a freelance hair consultant, and have worked in client-facing roles for the past eight years. During this time, I have worked my way up from a receptionist to a senior hair stylist, while simultaneously studying for my NVQ levels 1, 2 and 3.

Now, this brings me to why I am here today, interviewing with you.

I have always wanted to become cabin crew and, during the course of my career, I have been gradually mastering the skills needed to perform its tasks. I'm confident that the customer care and teamwork skills I have developed throughout the course of my career, combined with my friendly and positive nature, will complement your existing team and enable me to deliver the standard of service that passengers have come to expect from Fly High Airlines.

I'd now like to discuss how I might continue my success by joining your team."

Why should

WE HIRE YOU?

This is the time to shine, so don't be modest. Consider the experience and character traits that are most relevant and transferable to the position and explain how you have demonstrated these in the past.

Try it with the A.B.C formula...

A: Answer
"Because I am a good fit for the position."

B: Back it up
"As you can see from my résumé I have worked in client facing roles for the past eight years, so I am certainly qualified to perform the diverse requirements of this role. Also, the fact that I have been promoted through the ranks is a clear testament to my abilities and the confidence my manager had in me. More significantly, however, my character is tailored to the role. As you will have observed during the group assessments, I am a very welcoming and social individual who interacts well with others. I readily adapt to new people and environments, I am hard working and think fast on my feet."

C: Conclude
"I am confident that these aspects of my personality and experience will enable me to perform the job to the same high standard that exists currently and I believe I would be a valuable asset to your airline."

What are

YOUR BEST QUALITIES?

With this question, you need to read between the lines. The interviewer is not interested in your best qualities per se, but what qualities you have that would make you a good fit for the position. So tailor your answer to the requirements of the job and be sure to back it up with examples.

Try it with the A.B.C formula...

A: Answer
"As you will have observed during the group assessments, I am a very welcoming and social individual who interacts well with others, and readily adapts to new people and environments."

B: Back it up
"In fact, my previous supervisor also picked up on these attributes and often asked me to carry out the shampoo because she knew I would make the clients feel welcome and relaxed"

C: Conclude
"I am confident that these aspects of my character will enable me to perform the job to the same high standard that exists currently within the airline"

What is

YOUR GREATEST WEAKNESS?

The key to answering questions about weaknesses is to focus your response on those skills you are actively learning or planning to develop. This could be assertiveness or leadership. The point is, it is only a weakness because you haven't yet mastered it, and that is why you are working on developing those skills further. Be mindful, however, to not reveal weaknesses that are a major requiement fo the job.

Try it with the A.C.T formula...

A: Attack
"I recognise that my leadership ability is a potential area of improvement"

C: Clarify
"Which is why I am actively working on developing this area further through a part time training course at my local college"

T: Turn
"Although I am still learning, I see constant improvement in my capabilities when being faced with leadership tasks and I am confident that I will continue to learn and grow with experience"

Are you an introvert or extrovert?

"Actually, I would describe myself as an ambivert because I enjoy social interaction, but am equally happy to spend time alone in my own company."

What makes you stand out from the crowd?

"My friendly and positive nature certainly defines me as a person and makes me stand out from the crowd. I adopt a very optimistic view in every aspect of my life and refuse to allow external circumstances to negatively affect my state."

If you had to characterise yourself in one sentence, what would you say?

"I am a friendly and approachable person, who is sincere and very optimistic about life."

Rate yourself on a scale from 1 to 10

"I would rate myself as an 8. I always give my best, but in doing so I increase my skills. I, therefore, always see room for improvement."

How would a friend describe you?

"My friends would describe me as sociable, cheerful and optimistic. They would also say I am someone who thinks fast on my feet and stays calm in adverse situations."

How would an enemy describe your character?

"I suppose they might say that I am tenacious because I don't give in without a struggle, but am realistic about my limits. They might say I am brave because I am prepared to confront issues when there is a need, but I weigh the consequences and don't act irresponsibly. And, maybe, driven because I push for what I want, but can back off when advisable to do so."

How have you changed in the last five years?

"I feel like I have matured rather than aged five years. The skills I have acquired and the qualities I have developed have changed me enormously, and I know there are parts of me that are still not being utilised half as effectively as they could be. My customer care and communication skills have definitely been improved, and I have a better ability to use my initiative and think on my feet."

What is the importance of having good communication skills?

"The ability to speak clearly, listen actively and comprehend effectively is vital for our successful interaction with others, and continued growth."

How confident are you about addressing a group?

"I used to be nervous about speaking in front of a group, yet I found that preparation, practice and knowing my subject helped me overcome this, I now have no problem addressing a group."

Rate your communication skills on a scale of 1 to 10.

"I would rate myself as an 8. I always give my best, but in doing so I increase my skills. I, therefore, always see room for improvement."

Do you think your lack of language skills will affect your ability to perform the job?

"I admit my language skills are a little light, however, I am working on increasing my language fluency and, should I be offered the position, I will be sure to work on increasing my language abilities even further."

How would you define good customer service?

"Good customer service is about constantly and consistently meeting customer's expectations by providing a friendly, efficient and reliable service throughout the life of the service and/or product.

Excellent customer service is about exceeding customer's expectations by going beyond the call of duty. I believe that because no two customers are the same, they deserve to receive a service that is tailored to their individual needs. This is where a service moves beyond being just a satisfactory one, and becomes an excellent one."

What do you think constitutes poor customer service?

"Poor service is when customers are treated with disrespect and provided with a poor quality product and/or service by rude, ignorant and unhelpful staff."

Do you think the customer is always right?

"Whilst every customer is important, they are certainly not always right. Those who exhibit abusive behaviour, or do anything to compromise safety are straying beyond the boundary."

When have you witnessed good customer service?

"I remember when I visited a local restaurant for a luncheon. It had just turned 3pm on a Wednesday afternoon and, much to mine and the management's surprise, they were exceptionally busy with only three waiting staff on duty. Despite the overwhelming rush our waitress, Claire, was very polite and helpful. The staff showed great teamwork as they managed to pull together and deliver an outstanding service."

When have you witnessed poor customer service?

"I needed a particular material for a dress I was making. In most stores the salesperson would give me a quick 'no' before I finished explaining what I was looking for. I hadn't really noticed until I experienced the opposite service in another smaller fabric store."

What do you enjoy about providing customer care?

"The most enjoyable aspect I would have to say is that because I genuinely care about my client's satisfaction, it rewards me personally when I know that they are happy with the job I did. This, in turn, drives me to do better."

What do you dislike about providing customer care?

"Providing good customer care can be a challenge, and some people may view that negatively, but I view each challenge as an opportunity to develop and grow. So, because I am committed to developing myself, I welcome and enjoy the challenges of providing customer care. It is something I have become very good at."

What do you find most challenging about providing customer service?

"Providing customer service is a challenge in itself. Because people are unpredictable by their very nature, you have to always expect the unexpected and be prepared to go beyond the call of duty and deal with issues as they arrive."

How would you define teamwork?

"Teamwork is a group of people who work cooperatively together to achieve a common goal. They make a coordinated effort and each individual contributes their unique skills and ideas to the task."

Do you prefer to work alone or as part of a team?

"I am happy either way, and equally efficient at both. So, whether I prefer to work alone or in a team would depend on the best way to complete the job.

I do, however, have a preference towards team spirit. As well as the interaction, there is greater satisfaction when you share the joy of completing a task."

Are you a team player?

"Absolutely I am. As you will have observed during the group assessments, I interact well with others, and readily adapt to new people. I am a good listener, I respect other people's opinions and I can be relied on to contribute to the overall goal.

In fact, my previous supervisor used to say that my infectious optimism created excitement in other team members and resulted in a greater team effort and higher output."

What role do you assume in a team situation?

"I am whatever I need to be. If a situation comes up and someone needs to take charge, then I will. But if someone else has already taken charge and is solving it, I will follow their lead."

What do you enjoy about working as part of a team?

"There's nothing like being part of a great team where you can learn from the other members, bounce ideas off one another, and share achievements and rewards. There is a unique feeling of camaraderie that can never be experienced from working alone."

What do you least enjoy about working as part of a team?

"People not pulling their weight can be frustrating. However, I've noticed that such people simply lack enthusiasm or confidence, and that energetic and cheerful coworkers can often change that."

What do you find most challenging about being part of a team?

"The most challenging aspect is inspiring and motivating other team members. Each has different needs and is motivated by different things."

Are you happy to be supervised by people who are younger than yourself?

"Absolutely. I don't consider age to be an important factor. What matters is a person's credibility, professionalism and competency."

Why did you

LEAVE YOUR LAST JOB?

While you do need to be honest about your reasons for leaving past employment, you need to be diplomatic in your response. Being bored or not getting along with your boss are not ideal answers here. Be positive and be concise.

No opportunities
"While I enjoyed working for my previous employer, and appreciate the skills I developed while I was there, I felt I was not being challenged enough in the job. After working my way up through the company, there were no further opportunities for advancement."

Redundancy
"I survived the first layoffs, but unfortunately this one got me."

Note: Be prepared to be asked how many people were laid off.

Temporary post
"The job was only a temporary position, which I took to broaden my experience."

Never admit TO BEING FIRED

When it comes to lying, there is one exception to the rule and that is if you have a termination on your record. The recruiters will not care if the termination was unjust, unfair or has a good explanation, a termination is a big red flag and will mark the end of your interview so you need to do everything you can to avoid disclosing it.

In the first instance, you may choose to omit the information. Omitting details is not the same as telling an outright lie or making a false statement.

If you have just been fired from your most recent employment, they will not know unless you tell them. So you could mark your employment to present and leave it at that. If asked if they can call your employer for a reference, it would not raise any eyebrows if you respectfully decline due to your ongoing employment.

The third option is to take proactive measures to have the termination designation changed. If the termination occurred some time ago, it is more likely that the employer will be open to changing the designation if you accept responsibility and demonstrate a sincere regret for the situation. Simply advise them that the termination is damaging your chances of gaining employment and you would like the designation changed to something neutral, such as laid off or resigned.

If you would feel uncomfortable or unethical to omit such a detail and would prefer to take accountability for what happened, be sure to downplay the termination'. You will have some damage control to contend with, so remember to accept the mistake, don't blame others and don't make any excuses. Stick to the facts, point out what went wrong and what you have learned from the experience.

Whichever route you take, there is a risk. Either you will not be hired by admitting to the termination or you may not be hired because you did not disclose it and were caught out. The decision has to be yours.

Why were you
FIRED?

> If you choose to reveal your termination, be sure to accept the mistake, don't make excuses or blame others. Stick to the facts, point out what went wrong and what you have learnt from the experience.

Incompatibility
"I was desperate for work and took the job without fully understanding the expectations. It turned out that my competencies were not a right match for the employer's needs, so we agreed that it was time for me to move on to a position that would be more suitable. I certainly learnt a great deal from this experience and it's not a mistake I will ever repeat."

Personal reasons
"I had been going through a rough patch in my personal life which, unfortunately, upset my work life. It is regrettable and my circumstances have now changed, but I really wasn't in the position to avoid it at the time."

Immaturity
"I was a recent college graduate and didn't have the maturity and respect for work or a career that I now have. I have certainly grown up a lot since then, and I now understand what it is I want to do with my life."

Never:

» Badmouth previous employers, colleagues or bosses.

» Place blame

» Tell lies

» Reveal team incompatibility

Why have you

HAD SO MANY JOBS?

A fragmented work history will give the impression of a job hopper and will raise serious doubts about your commitment.

Whatever the reason, whether you have held temporary agency contracts, have been struggling to find something that you can feel committed to, or have simply been trying to gain a more rounded skill-set, it is important to put a positive spin on it, so that you can avoid any negative and rash assumptions being made.

Broaden experience
"I wanted to experience different jobs to broaden my knowledge, skills and experience. This has provided me with a very valuable and rounded skill set."

Temporary positions
"Due to the lack of full time opportunities in my area, I was only able to secure short term contracts."

Youth
In my youth, I was unsure about the direction I wanted to take in my career. I have matured a great deal since those days and am now interested in establishing myself into a long term opportunity.

What do you dislike
ABOUT YOUR CURRENT JOB?

There will always be less than exciting aspects of a job, however, being critical about your job isn't going to create a positive impression. So, soften these aspects as much as possible and try to select neutral examples, such as paperwork, lack of job security or opportunities for growth.

"I honestly can't think of any major dislikes. I don't think I'd be able to really excel if I weren't truly interested in the work, or if I were merely motivated by its financial rewards. I guess my answer will have to come under the category or nuisances.

The biggest nuisance is the paperwork. I realise the importance of documentation, and I cooperatively fill out the forms, but I'm always looking for efficiencies in that area that will get me out in front of the client where I belong."

Why were you
UNEMPLOYED FOR SO LONG?

It is better to say that you chose to take time off between jobs than it is to give the impression that you were unemployable.

Study
"I wanted to broaden my knowledge base, so I went back into full time study."

Travel
"I wanted to experience the world before settling into a long term career. I am now ready to commit."

Youth
"In my youth, I felt confused about the direction I wanted my career to take. I am now much more mature and certain in my desired direction."

Personal reasons
"Personal circumstances prohibited me from taking gainful employment, however, circumstances have now changed and I am ready to get back to work."

Why did you stay with the same employer for so long?

"I was there for several years, but in a variety of different roles. The opportunities for growth were fantastic so it felt as though I was undergoing frequent changes without actually changing employer. I didn't see the need to move on."

Why have you decided to change professions at this stage of your career?

"This career turnaround hasn't come suddenly. I have always wanted to become cabin crew and have been gradually mastering the skills needed to perform its tasks. I have now reached a point in my life where I am prepared to make the career and lifestyle change. I want to take advantage of that opportunity while it is presented to me."

What do you like about your current job?

"Rather than pick out the little details of the routine work, here are three general things. First is customer satisfaction. Seeing a client's face glow with happiness when their hair is transformed gives me an intense feeling of pride. Second is the interaction I get with my colleagues and clients. Finally, I enjoy being creative and finding new ways to please the customer."

Which particular aspect of your work do you find most frustrating?

"That's an interesting question because I am, generally speaking, a tolerant person. Slow periods can be sources of frustration, but at times like that I put more effort into advertising and establishing new clientele. That way, the slow periods don't last long."

What contribution can you make to ensure passengers will fly with us again?

My customer service experience and friendly character style will enable me to deliver a superior standard of service which will make passengers feel welcome, valued and relaxed.

Why should we hire you instead of someone with cabin crew experience?

"Although I might not have cabin crew experience, I have the necessary skills to make an impressive start, and the willingness to learn and improve. Sometimes, employers do better when they hire people who don't have a great deal of repetitive experience. That way, they can train these employees in their methods and ways of doing the job. Training is much easier than untraining."

Why should we hire you for this position rather than another applicant?

"I can't tell you why you should hire me instead of another candidate but, I can tell you why you should hire me."

Are you willing to start as a trainee?

"Yes, absolutely. This is a new area for me, and I believe in getting a good foundation in the basics before progressing. An entry level position will enable me to learn the position inside out, and will give me the opportunity to grow when I prove myself. I also have a great deal of knowledge and work experience, which I'm sure will contribute to my successful progression through training."

How do you feel about the probationary period?

"I can see no problem with a probationary period. I am a fast learner so it shouldn't take me long to prove myself."

How do you feel about working at Christmas, and other special occasions?

"Naturally, I would miss spending time with my friends and family, but my career is important to me and my family and friends respect and appreciate that fact. I am happy to make the sacrifice as necessary."

How do you feel about a formal dress code?

"I have always liked to dress formally and feel very comfortable wearing formal attire. I realise that a standard of dress is necessary in order to project a professional image to the passengers."

This is a long hours culture, is that a problem for you?

"I understand that this a demanding job, but I really do thrive on the challenge of this sort of work and have worked long hours in the past, so I am willing to work whatever hours are necessary to get the work done."

This position will involve relocating, how will you adjust to the different lifestyle?

"I realise that this position involves transfers, and I bore that in mind when I applied. I am fully aware of what to expect from the research I have done and would welcome the different lifestyle."

How do you feel about the routine tasks and irregular hours of this job?

"I accept that every role carries with it a certain amount of routine in order to get the job done. If my job involves repetitive work, it is my responsibility to carry it out to the best of my abilities. As for irregular hours I would expect to have an indication of my core hours, but will work the hours that are necessary in order to fulfil the requirements of the role."

Do you feel confident in your ability to handle this position?

"Yes, absolutely. I'm very confident in my abilities. I'm familiar with the basic job requirements and I learn quickly. It undoubtedly will take time and effort on my part, but I'm more than willing to devote that time and effort."

Do you feel ready for a more responsible position?

"Absolutely. I believe that eight years experience working closely with customers, has prepared me professionally and personally to move up to this role. My customer care and teamwork skills have been finely tuned over the years, and I know I am capable of greater achievements."

How will you cope with the change in environment?

"I welcome the challenge of learning about and adapting to a new environment, that's one of the reasons I'm seeking to make a career change right now. Any major change, while always containing some challenge is a chance to grow, learn, and advance."

Do you work well under pressure?

"Absolutely. Because pressure is the result of a new challenge, I perceive pressure as an opportunity to develop and grow. The more challenges I experience, the better my skills become, and the less I feel the pressure of subsequent challenges. So, because I am committed to developing myself, I welcome the challenges of pressure."

How would I know you were under pressure?

"I disguise my pressure well, therefore, I would hope that it wouldn't be obvious enough to notice."

What types of people annoy you or try your patience?

"That's an interesting question, because I am a very tolerant person. However, there are instances where my patience is put to the test, but I am able to control myself and my emotions, so I never let my patience move beyond the testing stage."

Do you have difficulties tolerating people with different views than you?

"No. I recognise that everyone has their own views, and that they may not always correspond with my own. Differing views and personalities are what make us individual, so I don't let other people's views or interests affect how I feel about them."

How often do you lose your temper?

"I never lose my temper. I regard that sort of behaviour as counterproductive and inappropriate. By losing your temper, you cannot possibly resolve a problem. Even if you're completely right, losing your temper often destroys your ability to convince others of this."

What makes you angry or impatient?

"Anger to me means loss of control, and I'm not the kind of person who loses control. It is counterproductive and inappropriate, and doesn't gain anything of value.

When I feel stress building up, instead of getting angry or impatient, I take a deep breath and begin to focus on the positives. The results are quite dramatic, my whole demeanour changes very rapidly,"

How do you handle criticism?

"As long as the criticism is fair and constructive, I listen to it and remain gracious. I thank them for their candid feedback, express regret over the situation and modify my future behaviour accordingly."

DETERMINING YOUR COMPETENCIES

1 When have you gone out of your way for a customer?

Evaluation

Those candidates who demonstrate that they always put in extra effort to provide a better and more complete service will surely have an advantage.

Your answer should demonstrate that you always go the extra mile, and never deliver a merely acceptable standard.

Sample Response 1

Situation:
I had a client call into the store who was looking for a very specific style of fabric. She had visited several stores in and around the area but hadn't been successful in her search.

I could see that she was exhausted, but also very determined. She spoke with such sorrow in her voice that I actually began to feel sorry for the poor lady because I didn't have the fabric to sell her.

Action:
Not wanting to be the bearer of more bad news, I decided to offer my assistance. I spent several hours ringing around wholesalers, distributors and manufacturers trying to track down this particular fabric, when finally I struck gold with a small manufacturing plant.

Result:
Because the fabric was a special order, there was a small handling charge, but the customer received the fabric within a few days and was sure it was worth the expense and wait.

Sample Response 2

Situation:
I encountered a problem when one of my clients was unable to have a hair treatment carried out in her home because it was being renovated.

Action:
In an attempt to keep the client, I spoke to a contact I had within a local salon and was able to negotiate a small fee for use of the salon facilities.

Result:
This worked out really well because it was convenient for both myself and the client to travel to. Since then, I have negotiated similar deals with four other salons and have increased my customer base dramatically as a direct result.

2 Describe a time when your customer service could have been better?

Evaluation

Providing excellent customer service is vital, so you should be very cautious when providing negative examples.

You could take a modest approach and explain that you always strive to do better, or you could be honest with humble example.

Alternatively, you could attempt to avoid providing an example by explaining how you maintain your standards, and then proceed with an example of a time when you have demonstrated this capability.

Sample Response (Modest approach)

I take great pride in providing the best service I possibly can, but in doing so I increase my skills and can always see room for improvement.

Sample Response (No experience)

I take great pride in providing the best service I possibly can, and I never let my standards slip. Even during times of high pressure, I make an effort to remain courteous and helpful. I can honestly say that I have never received any negative feedback.

3 When have you solved a customer problem?

Evaluation

The recruiter wants to get an idea of how you apply your initiative and problem-solving skills to customer related issues. A good answer here will demonstrate that you always put in extra effort to provide good customer service and are not intimidated by difficult situations.

Sample Response

Situation:
I remember a client who came to me to have her hair extensions replaced. She had worn sewn in extensions for several months and was experiencing some discomfort from the attachments.

Action:
As I examined her hair, I was shocked to discover how much damage had been caused. Her roots had become severely matted and the tightness from the installed tracks had created spots of baldness.

I took a moment to analyse the situation, work out a strategy and then I set to work.

I spent several hours meticulously untangling every hair and removing every extension piece, The more I removed, the more I could see the scale of the damage that had been caused. Sadly, the client's hair was in very bad shape after the removal and the spots of baldness were very evident. Needless to say, I had a very emotional customer.

I applied a very deep conditioning protein treatment to the customers remaining locks and gave it a good trim. I then finished up with some fine and strategically placed fusion hair extensions to conceal the bald patches and create some much needed volume.

Result:
Following the treatment, the client looked fantastic and her smile was restored. Her hair soon returned to its former glory and she became a regular client of mine.

4 When have you tended to an upset customer?

Evaluation

The recruiter is trying to grasp your ability to cope with stressful situations. A good answer will suggest that you can think on your feet, and display a positive and patient attitude when challenging situations arise.

Sample Response

Situation:
I recently experienced a situation with a client who was having relationship problems. She was becoming increasingly emotional and I could sense that she was feeling very depressed.

Action:
Although I felt compassion for her situation, I knew that it was important for me not to get overly involved. So, I gave her chance to talk while I listened, and I tried to show empathy while remaining neutral and professional in my response.

Result:
Just being able to talk to someone who listened seemed to make her feel better. As she continued to speak, she appeared to have gained a deeper insight into her situation and actually began seeing things more positively. Consequently, she was able to calmly discuss her feelings with her partner and work through their problems. She later thanked me for listening.

Reflection:
From this experience, I learned that just listening can be providing good customer care.

5 Have you been confronted by an aggressive customer?

Evaluation

The ability to remain well-mannered and well-tempered while dealing with an aggressive customer is an absolute necessity. The recruiter will want to assess whether you can deal with confrontational issues in a calm and rational manner.

You will be assessed on how well you coped under the pressure and how you dealt with the customer. A good response will show that you never lost your temper and remained courteous throughout the experience.

Sample Response

Situation:
Shortly after I began freelancing, I encountered a problem when an associate of mine tried to pressure me into a free service based on friendship.

Action:
I proceeded to offer her, what I considered to be, a reasonable discount, but she was not satisfied with my offer and proceeded to pressure me with emotional blackmail. I remained cordial, but became more assertive as I continued to refuse her demands.

Result:
Rather than accept the reasons for my decision, she became increasingly enraged, and even began to slander my service and friendship

Shocked at her over-reaction, and concerned about what might develop, I felt I had no option but to withdraw from the situation.

Reflection:
This experience was very challenging and certainly tested my patience. But I remained calm and, although this particular relationship never recovered, it was a learning experience that hasn't since been repeated.

6 When have you had to say 'No' to a customer?

Evaluation

There will be occasions when it is necessary to say no to a passenger. The recruiter wants to know that you aren't intimidated by such situations and have the strength of character to deal with the situation authoritatively, yet diplomatically.

You will be assessed on how you approached the customer and went about dealing with the situation. A good response will demonstrate your ability to use tact, and will show that you remained courteous throughout the experience.

Sample Response

Situation:
I remember when a customer tried to return a pair of trainers to the store for a refund. Although the customer denied it, I could see that the shoes had clearly been worn.

Action:
I remained calm and polite as I suggested that the shoes could not be returned unless faulty or unused.

The customer become very aggressive and repeatedly threatened to contact our head office to complain about me if I didn't refund him immediately.

I remained assertive and suggested this would be the best course of action for him to take. I then proceeded to provide him with the full details of our complaints manager within the head office.

Result:
Realising defeat, the man stormed out of the shop and, to my knowledge, never did take the matter further.

7 When have you handled a customer complaint?

Evaluation

The recruiter wants to know that you are able to retain your composure and use your problem solving skills when dealing with a dissatisfied customer.

A good response will show that you never took the complaint personally, remained calm and courteous, and were able to create a satisfactory outcome for the customer.

Sample Response

Situation:
I remember when a customer complained about a meal they had purchased.

Because over two thirds of the entire course had been eaten, not only was it obvious that the complaint was insincere, but it was also against the restaurants policy to offer a refund under such circumstances.

The customer was becoming very enraged and threatened to write to the trading standards and newspapers if I did not give him a full refund.

Action:
I gave the customer my undivided attention while he vented his frustrations. Then, when he had finally calmed down, I calmly apologised for the dissatisfaction and proceeded to offer a meal deal voucher as a goodwill gesture.

Result:
The customer was clearly unhappy not to have received a refund, but he left the restaurant and, as suspected, never did take the matter any further.

8 When have you had to resolve a conflict between what the customer wanted and what you could realistically deliver?

Evaluation

The recruiter wants to determine that you have the strength of character to voice your concerns. They also want to see that you can be diplomatic, yet authoritative, in your communication style.

You will be assessed on how you approached the customer and how you dealt with the situation.

Sample Response

Situation:
I remember a client who came to me for a colour treatment and restyle. She had used a virtual hairstyle software to create her ideal look and was beaming with excitement as she showed me the picture.

The style was notably very pretty, and it was clear that it was ideally suited to the client. Unfortunately, however, the client's hair had been through several perming and colour treatments, and the platinum blonde shade that she wanted just wasn't going to be possible at that time.

Action:
Knowing how excited the client was, I felt a little dejected as I proceeded to break this news to her. In the hope of relieving some of her obvious disappointment, I suggested a strand test to see if it would be possible to lift some of the colour without causing excessive damage. If the strand test were a success, we could perform a gradual transformation through the use of highlights.

Result:
Thankfully, the strand test was a success and the client, while naturally disappointed, was happy to go ahead with the gradual transformation. The result was striking,and the client was happy with the result.

Within nine months, the transformation was complete, and I had a very satisfied customer.

9 Describe a situation when the customer was wrong

Evaluation

Although the popular saying suggests otherwise, the customer isn't always right and the recruiter wants to know that you aren't Intimidated by such situations.

You will be assessed on how you approached the customer and went about dealing the situation. A good response will demonstrate your ability to use tact, and will show that you remained courteous throughout the experience.

Sample Response

Situation:
I remember a client who I had carried out a perming treatment for. After completing the treatment, I provided written instructions for how to care for her new perm which specifically instructed against washing the hair for at least 48 hours.

Unfortunately, the very next day the client washed her hair and the perm dropped out. The client was understandably very upset, but refused to accept that the perm had fallen out as a consequence of her own actions. She became very irate and started to slander my work and the salon.

Action:
When asked if she had followed the instructions, she denied being provided with any. I assured her that instructions were provided, and suggested she check her belongings.

Result:
Later that afternoon, the client returned to the salon holding onto the instruction sheet with a very embarrassed look on her face. She apologised profusely for her behaviour.

Reflection:
To avoid a repeat of this situation, I now provide clearer warnings within the written information sheet and back it up with verbal instructions.

10 Have you ever bent the rules for a customer?

Evaluation

There are situations where it is permissible to bend the rules, however, some airlines may view rule bending very negatively. So, no matter how trivial or well-intended, you may want to play it safe and declare that you have never gone against the rules.

If you do decide to provide an answer, you should show that you are able to keep balance between company policy and the interest of customers.

Sample Response

I have always abided by company policies and have never bent the rules. Bending the rules for one customer, will no doubt lead to a downward spiral . Either the customer will expect further rule bending, or other customers will catch on and expect the same treatment. It's just not a wise course of action to take.

11 Tell me about a time when you failed to communicate effectively?

Evaluation

We all experience challenges in communication, but a complete failure to communicate effectively will show a lack of initiative and creativity in problem solving.

Whatever the reason for a communication challenge, there is always a way to communicate if you are willing to put in some additional effort. Your answer should reflect this.

Sample Response (Modest Approach)

While I have certainly encountered communication challenges, I can honestly say that I have never yet completely failed in my ability to communicate. With some creativity, I have always found a way to overcome communication barriers.

Sample Response (Humble Example)

Situation:
Generally, I am a very efficient communicator, but I do recall when I experienced difficulty communicating with an OAP client.

Action:
The client was very hard of hearing, and I tried everything to communicate with her. I spoke slower, louder, used hand gestures and facial expressions, I even tried to write the information down, but without her glasses she was unable see my writing clearly.

Result:
Fortunately, I managed to locate a magnifying glass, which enabled the client to read my instructions, and everything worked out well in the end.

12 When have your communication skills made a difference to a situation or outcome?

Evaluation

The ability to communicate well is vital to the role of cabin crew, so you should have plenty of real life examples ready to share. This is your chance to shine, so don't be modest.

Sample Response

Situation:
I remember a trainee apprentice we had in our department who never asked questions and refused all offers of help. Unfortunately, instead of trying to understand her reasons, everyone drew the conclusion that she was a know-it-all and vowed not to offer help in the future.

Action:
Concerned that her progress would suffer, I decided to offer my encouragement and support. It soon became evident from our conversation that she had excessively high expectations of herself and feared looking incompetent. I explained that it was okay to ask questions, and mistakes were expected. I even shared a few of my own early mishaps to lighten the mood.

Result:
Very quickly after that we saw a change in her behaviour. She began asking questions, she was more open to suggestions, and her skills improved immensely.

Reflection:
From this experience, I learnt that things are not always what they appear and we need to be more objective before making rash judgements.

13 Give an example of when you had to present complex information in a simplified manner in order to explain it to others

Evaluation

As cabin crew, you may be required to break down and convey complex information to customers. For example, if a passenger is afraid of flying, you may need to explain the technicalities of the flight, or if a passenger is hasn't grasped the use of emergency equipment and emergency procedures, you may need to break the information down further.

Your answer here should show that you are able to express knowledge in a clear and simple manner.

Sample Response

Situation:
I remember a client who was interested in having a colour treatment carried out. She was very inquisitive and asked numerous questions, so I could sense that she was concerned about the process and potential damage to her natural hair.

Action:
Not satisfied with a simple nontechnical version, I had to provide a detailed technical breakdown of the whole process. This involved describing the molecular structure of the hair, the effect colour particles have and how they bond to the structure.

Result:
Although I had to occasionally refer to training manuals to emphasise or clarify my point, overall the client was satisfied with my effort. As a direct result, she went ahead with the treatment and was very pleased with the outcome.

14 Have you ever had to overcome a language barrier?

Evaluation

As cabin crew, you will interact with a variety of people from a broad range of cultures and backgrounds. The ability to relate to others and adapt your communication style is, therefore, very important.

Sample Response

Situation:
During a trip to Africa, I became acquainted with a French lady. She understood my French, the little amount I knew, but she didn't really understand English. Unfortunately, the amount of French I knew wasn't enough to get me through a whole conversation, so I had to improvise.

Action:
I spoke French wherever possible and filled in the gaps with improvised sign language and facial expressions.

Result:
At first it was a little tricky trying to find imaginative ways to communicate, but over time I became much more proficient. I'm sure she was amused by my amateur efforts, but it worked out well and I came away with a new friend.

Reflection:
Now when I encounter this type of communication barrier, I am much more confident in my ability to cope.

15 Tell me about a time that you had to work as part of a team

Evaluation

The ability to work well within a team is absolutely essential to working as cabin crew. You should, therefore, have plenty of examples that demonstrate this ability.

Sample Response

Situation:
There was a particular time that stands out for me because it was such an unusual occurrence.

It was a usual quiet Tuesday afternoon and only myself, the senior stylist, an apprentice, and the salon manager were on duty. To our surprise, it was as if someone started offering out free chocolate, as clients started to filter through the doors.

Action:
Despite the overwhelming rush, we showed great teamwork as we pulled together and shared our duties. Even our manager showed great team spirit as she got involved with the hair service.

Result:
As a result of our teamwork, and some free relaxing conditioning treatments, we managed to deliver an outstanding service. Every client went away completely satisfied.

16 When have you struggled to fit in?

Evaluation

With the constant rotation of crew, there will be some people that you don't immediately hit it off with. The recruiters want to know that you aren't intimidated by such difficulties and are able to move past any struggles.

Sample Response

Situation:
When I started working at Trina's Hair & Beauty, I was joining a very close-knit team who had been together for a number of years.

As a result of the number of trainees they had witnessed come and go over the years, they had become a little reluctant to accept new trainees.

I wouldn't say it was a struggle to fit in as such, but I certainly experienced some growing pains. With remarks such as 'if you are still here then' to contend with, I knew I had to prove myself.

Action:
To show that I was serious about the job, and was not a fly-by-night, I focused a lot of effort on learning my new job. At the same time, I continued to be friendly and respectful of my new colleagues while I made a conscious effort to get to know them.

Result:
As a result of my hard effort, It didn't take long for them to accept me and include me as part of their team. Naturally, I have become closer to some of my colleagues than with others, but we all got on and worked well as a team.

17 Have you ever experienced difficulties getting along with colleagues?

Evaluation

No matter how hard we try, or how likeable we are, there will always be someone that we don't hit it off with. To say otherwise, would not sound credible.

For the most part, this question is asked to determine your ability to get along with other people and manage adversity. The recruiters want to know that you don't allow conflict to interfere with work.

The best answer should show that you aren't intimidated or confrontational in such situations, but you put in the commitment necessary to build a respectful and healthy working relationship.

Sample Response

Situation:
I remember one co-worker in particular who flat out didn't like me. It didn't matter what I did or said, or whether I tried to avoid or befriend this person.

Action:
After a couple of days of subtle hostility, I decided to assert myself. I diplomatically explained that I acknowledged her dislike for me and I asked for input as to what I must do to create a professional relationship

Result:
Although we never became friends, we were able to maintain more cordial relations thereafter.

18 Tell us about a challenge you have faced with a colleague

Evaluation

Airlines have a constant rotation of crew on-board each aircraft and, especially within larger airlines, you may not work with the same crew members twice. As a result, it is guaranteed that you will encounter challenging situations with colleagues.

The recruiters want to know that you aren't intimidated by such colleagues or situations, and are prepared to use your initiative to diffuse or mediate as necessary to keep working relationships healthy.

Your answer should demonstrate your willingness to cooperate with others to resolve differences, improve relations, and manage conflicts. It should also display your ability to remain patient and positive in the face of adversity.

Sample Response

Situation:
I do remember one situation where two of my colleagues really didn't hit it off with one another. They were constantly quarrelling and everyone had lost patience with them, but no one wanted to get involved.

Action:
In the end, I decided to take the initiative and act as a sort of mediator to the situation. I was not their manager, so I had to be as tactful as I could so that I wouldn't upset anyone.

I started by explaining that I acknowledged their dislike for each other and then I drew upon the fact that they are both professionals and can, therefore, put aside their differences for the good of the team.

Result:
They had a pretty frank discussion and, although I can't say they ended up the best of friends, they did work out an effective strategy for working more productively together.

19 Tell me about a disagreement with a colleague

Evaluation

We all have disagreements with colleagues, but they should never get out of control or interfere with work.

You may choose to disclose the details of a conflict situation, but make sure it was minor and didn't interfere with work. Conversely, you may wish to play it safe and declare that while you have had disagreements, they were so minor that you don't really recall the exact details. You could then go on to reiterate some minor examples.

The recruiters want to know that you aren't intimidated by conflicts and have the ability to see things from another person's perspective. Your answer should demonstrate that you are prepared to use your initiative and interpersonal skills to improve relations with colleagues, even in cases where they cannot agree upon certain issues.

Sample Response

Introduction:
Working in a creative environment with other highly skilled professionals, it was natural that we had the occassional clash of ideas. Any disagreements we did have, however, were so relatively minor and insignificant that I would be hard pressed to recall the exact details.

Situation:
Our disagreements were usually as a result of our individual preference towards certain products, styles, magazines or equipment.

Action:
Our debates were never confrontational and they never interfered with our work in any way.

Result:
In fact, some very interesting views emerged from these debates which sometimes resulted in people, including myself, having a slight change in my perspective. So, they were often very educational.

20 Have you successfully worked with a difficult coworker?

Evaluation

The recruiters want to know that you aren't intimidated by difficult colleagues or situations, and are prepared to use your initiative to deal with the situation as necessary. You will be assessed on how you approached the colleague and how you dealt with the situation.

Your answer should demonstrate your willingness to co-operate with others to resolve differences, improve relations, and manage conflicts. It should also display your ability to remain patient and positive when challenging situations occur.

Sample Response

Situation:
I remember one member of staff was always complaining. Nothing was ever good enough or couldn't possibly work. Everyone had lost patience with her but, because she was so incredibly sensitive, no one said anything.

Action:
I spent some time with her and tactfully told her that it appeared as if she was always putting our ideas down.

Result:
On hearing this feedback she was genuinely horrified at her own behaviour. She explained that she hadn't realised it had made everyone feel that way and agreed that from then on she would try to be more positive.

Very quickly after that we saw a change in her behaviour. She became more conscious of her own attitude and deliberately tried to be more considerate. From that point on, no one could have hoped for a more committed team member.

21 Have you ever worked with someone you disliked?

Evaluation

There will always be someone that we don't like and to try to convince the recruiter otherwise would not sound honest or credible.

For the most part, this question is asked to determine your ability to get along with other people and manage adversity. The recruiters want to know that you don't allow personal views cause conflict or interfere with work.

The best answer should show that you aren't intimidated or confrontational in such situations, but you put in the commitment necessary to build a respectful and healthy working relationship

Sample Response

Situation:
There was one colleague I worked with that I really found it difficult to get along with personally.

Action:
Instead of focusing on those things I didn't like, I put my personal views aside and focused on the skills she brought to the position.

Result:
My personal view of her never changed, and we never became friends, but we did work productively alongside each other without any problems.

22 Have you ever acted as a mentor to a coworker?

Evaluation

There may be times when you have to mentor new crew members and the recruiters are trying to assess your ability to lead and mentor your colleagues.

Sample Response

Situation:
I remember when one of our trainees was having problems understanding certain aspects of her course material, and I could see she was becoming increasingly frustrated and self critical.

Action:
Having witnessed her in action, I knew that she was a very bright and talented individual with no obvious lack of skill. So, I determined that her frustrations were probably the result of the pressure she was feeling about her approaching exam.

Concerned at the effect this pressure was having on her, and having experienced the same pressures myself, I decided to offer my support. To reinforce her understanding, I demonstrated some of the techniques she had been struggling with and showed her a few memory tips and tricks which had helped me through my exams.

Result:
My breakdown of the processes, along with the visual demonstration I provided, seemed to make the material much more understandable for her. In the days that followed, she seemed to have a new lease of life and was much more positive. Subsequently, she passed her exams with top grades.

23 What have you done that shows initiative?

Evaluation

Your answer here should show that you take the initiative when it comes to additional work and demonstrate a natural desire for doing extra tasks willingly.

Sample Response

Situation:
When I began working for my current employer, the inventory system was outdated and the storage room was very messy and disorganised.

Action:
I came in on my day off, cleaned up the mess, organised the store cupboards and catalogued it all on the new inventory forms.

Result:
Thereafter, when orders arrived it was easy to organise and retrieve.

Reflection:
If I'm able to do the task, instead of waiting for the job to be done, I simply do it.

24 Have you undertaken a course of study, on your own initiative, in order to improve your work performance?

Evaluation

Your answer here should show that you are committed to self-development and take the initiative when it comes to improving yourself and your efficiency.

Sample Response

Situation:
While at Trina's Hair Salon, we were experiencing a spectacular rise in demand for high fashion cuts. I had some creative cutting experience, but nothing that extended to the kind of advanced skill that was required for true high fashion cuts.

Action:
After some consideration, I decided that increasing my creative cutting skills would not only give the salon a competitive advantage, but it would also be a fantastic opportunity for me to move my skills to the next level. So, I took the initiative and, under my own funding, immediately enrolled onto a creative cutting course.

Result:
My new skills proved to be an instant success. Existing clients began recommending me to their friends, which resulted in a massive rise in clientele. Needless to say, my manager was very happy.

25 Describe an improvement that you personally initiated

Evaluation

The recruiter wants to know that you seek better and more effective ways of carrying out your work and can suggest improvements that will achieve more efficiency.

Your answer here should show that you take the initiative when it comes to improving working methods and standards.

Sample Response

Situation:
While travelling in India, I learnt the art of Indian head massage.

Action:
When I returned to work, I began using my new skill on clients while carrying out the shampoo.

Result:
My massages were becoming such a success, that my manager approached me to request that I train my colleagues. Naturally, I was honoured to oblige.

26 Describe a new idea or suggestion that you made to your supervisor

Evaluation

The recruiter wants to know that you aren't afraid to take the initiative and suggest improvements.

Sample Response

Situation:
When I was working at Trina's Hair Salon, I had noticed that a lot of our clients wore nail extensions.

Action:
Convinced that the service would be an improvement to our already successful salon, I carried out extensive independent research before presenting the idea to my manager.

Result:
After carrying out her own research, she liked the idea so much that she decided to go ahead with the new service. Within a couple of months, the service was up and running, and we experienced a dramatic increase in new clientele and revenue. I even got a small bonus in my pay packet for my involvement.

27 Tell me about a problem you encountered and the steps you took to overcome it

Evaluation

The recruiter will be assessing how well you cope with diverse situations, and how you use your judgment and initiative to solve problems.

In answering this question, you need to provide a concrete example of a problem you faced, and then Itemize the steps you took to solve the problem. Your answer should demonstrate a patient and positive attitude towards problem solving.

Sample Response

Situation:
Early in my freelancing career, I experienced several clients who turned up late to their appointments. Some even forgot about their appointments altogether. Rather than just simply being an inconvenience, it was wasting my time and money.

Action:
I considered my options and decided that the best solution would be to send out reminder cards a few days prior to client appointments. For the repeat offenders, I would enforce a late cancellation fee.

Result:
This decision drastically cut the number of late arrivers, and I have never since had a no-show.

28 Tell me about a problem that didn't work out

Evaluation

No matter how hard we try, there are some instances where a problem just doesn't work out. To say otherwise will not sound honest or credible.

In answering this question, you need to first ensure that the problem was a minor one which had no negative or lasting impact on the company, a colleague or a customer. Try to accentuate the positives and keep your answer specific. Itemize the steps you took to deal with the problem and make it clear that you learnt from the experience.

Sample Response

Situation:
Shortly after I began freelancing, my bank returned a client's cheque to me through lack of funds.

Action:
At first, I was sure it was a mistake caused through an oversight on the part of my client. I made a number of calls, left several messages and even attempted a visit to the clients home, all to no avail.

Several weeks passed and it was clear that I was chasing a lost cause. At this point, I had to decide whether to write off the debt and blacklist the client or visit the Citizens' Advice for advice on retrieving the funds.

Result:
After careful consideration of all the factors involved, I decided to write the debt off as a learning experience.

Reflection:
In hindsight, I realise it was a silly mistake that could easily have been avoided. I have never repeated this error since as I now wait for the funds to clear before carrying out a service.

29 Have you ever taken the initiative to solve a problem that was above your responsibilities?

Evaluation

Those candidates who demonstrate that they use their initiative and put in extra effort to provide a better and more complete service will surely be looked upon favourably.

Sample Response

Situation:
It had been quite an uneventful afternoon when, all of the sudden, in walked an obviously frantic customer.

From what I could understand, her laptop had contracted a virus while connected to the internet and the system now failed to respond to any commands.

Being a self-employed web designer, the customer was naturally very concerned about the potential loss of data, and earnings.

Unfortunately, while the laptop was still within warranty, it was beyond the companies scope and had to be sent to the manufacturer for restoration. My colleagues, while polite, but could only offer assistance as far as sending the laptop to the manufacturer.

Action:
I could sense the customer was becoming increasingly distressed and, having had previous training in system restoration, I was confident that I could at least safely extract the data from the hard drive.

After talking the customer through the procedure, she granted her permission and I proceeded.

Result:
After some 45 minutes of fiddling with wires and hard drives, the customer's data had been successfully, and safely, extracted. The customer gasped a big sigh of relief as we packaged the laptop off to the manufacturer for repair.

Several weeks later, my line manager received a letter from the customer complimenting my efforts.

Reflection:
I was really pleased that a little effort made such a big difference.

30 When have you made a bad decision?

Evaluation

We all make decisions that we regret, and to say otherwise will not sound honest or credible.

The recruiter will be assessing whether you have the character to admit and take responsibility for your mistake, whether your decision had a negative impact on customers or the company, and whether you learnt from this mistake?

In answering this question, you need to first ensure that the mistake was a minor one, which had no negative or lasting impact on the company, a colleague or a customer. Try to accentuate the positives and keep your answer specific. Itemize what you did and how you did it. Finally, you need to make it clear that you leant from the mistake and will be certain not to repeat it.

Situation:

Early in my freelance career, I was approached by a salesman who was promoting a protein conditioning system. He described the system as "The newest technology to emerge from years of research. Guaranteed to help heal, strengthen, and protect".

Although I was excited by the concept, I did have my concerns that the system sounded too good to be true. However, the salesman had all the official paperwork to back up his claims, and the literature was thorough and well presented. All these things, combined with the company's full money-back guarantee, made it appear to be a win-win situation, and a risk worth taking. So I invested.

Following my investment, I decided to test the system out on training heads before taking the system public. Unfortunately, several months of using the system passed with no obvious benefits.

Action:

Disappointed with the product, I decided to pursue the full money back guarantee, but the sales number was not recognised, and my letters were returned unopened. Even their website had mysteriously vanished. I soon came to the realisation that I had been taken in by an elaborate scam.

I contacted the Citizens Advice Bureau and Trading Standards, but there was little they could do to retrieve my funds.

Result:

Unfortunately, I never recovered my costs and had to put the mistake down to a learning experience.

Reflection:

Unfortunately, it really was my fault. I should have trusted my gut instinct and carried out thorough research before making my decision. It is a mistake I shall never repeat.

31 What was the biggest challenge you have faced?

Evaluation

In answering this question, you need to provide a concrete example of a challenge you faced, and then Itemize the steps you took to overcome that challenge.

Your answer should display a patient and positive attitude when challenging situations occur.

Sample Response

Situation:
To be honest, giving up smoking was the biggest challenge. I never thought I could do it, and I had made dozens of attempts that ended in failure.

Action:
Determined not to give in to my withdrawals, I decided I needed an incentive that would pull me through the tough times. Being sponsored for a worthy cause was the perfect solution.

Result:
With a good cause in mind, the following three months were easier than on previous occasions. Not only have I come out the other end a non-smoker, I also managed to raise £2464.00 for Childline.

Reflection:
Since I gave up smoking, I have gained so much personal insight, and I deal with potentially stressful situations at work so much more effectively now, I feel more energetic, more mentally alert and far calmer now than I ever did before.

HYPOTHETICAL & ROLE PLAY SCENARIOS

Hypothetical

Hypothetical questions present candidates with difficult real-life situations, where almost any answer can be challenged.

A good way to approach these questions is to consider the feelings of everyone involved, and think about the implications for your colleagues and the airline.

Prove to the recruiters that you would be proactive and do your best to resolve the situation using your own initiative, whilst remembering that you could ask for the help of the more experienced crew if necessary.

If you have followed these guidelines and are still challenged, the recruiter may be testing your ability to manage conflict or stress. Bear in mind that if you are not cabin crew yet, you cannot really be expected to know the best reply so do not be tricked into entering into an argument with the recruiter.

In either case it is important to remain calm and focused, and to demonstrate that, although you appreciate there are many aspects to each situation, you would always be trying to find acceptable solutions.

If you really can't think of a solution, you can simply say, "That is a new area for me so I am afraid I can't really answer that, but I enjoy acquiring new knowledge and I do learn quickly."

You are in flight at 30,000 feet. How would you handle a passenger if he became irate about his lost baggage?

"At 30,000 feet, there is not a lot you can do about the baggage, so the problem at hand is reassuring the passenger and avoiding further disruption.

First, I would try to manoeuvre the passenger somewhere more private where they can explain the situation. I would then apologise for the mishandling, and offer to assist on the ground by escorting him to the proper people who can help."

What would you do if the seat belt signs are on due to turbulence, but a passenger gets up to go to the toilet?

"Because of the importance of passenger safety, I would advise the passenger to wait until the seat belt signs have been turned off. If the passenger really cannot wait, I will follow the corporate policy for dealing with such a situation."

How would you handle a passenger who is intoxicated?

"I would not provide any more alcoholic beverages. I would encourage food, and offer a cup of tea or coffee. If the situation worsens beyond my control, I would inform my senior and seek assistance from the other crew members."

What would you do if a commercially important passenger complained about a crying child?

"I would apologise to the passenger and offer my assistance to the guardian of the child."

How would you deal with a passenger who is scared of flying?

"Being aware of what to expect, and just realising that a plane's wings are supposed to flex and move around gently in flight, can help relieve anxiety. Similarly, the collection of bumps and bangs that always accompany a flight can be made less fearsome if they are expected. So, I would try to comfort the passenger by talking them through the flight, and reassuring them of any strange noises they may hear.

I would advise them where I can be found, and show them the call bell. I would then check on them periodically throughout the flight."

How would you deal with a passenger who is not, right but believes he is right?

"I would explain the company's rules and policies to the passenger in a calm, professional and positive manner. Hopefully, this should clarify any misconceptions that the passenger may have."

How would you handle a colleague who is being rude or racist?

"I would act immediately to put a stop to any racist or rude behaviour by making it clear to the person that their behaviour is not acceptable. If he or she continues, I would then report it to proper authority."

If you spotted a colleague doing something unethical or illegal, what would you do?

"I would act immediately to put a stop to any unethical or illegal activity. I would try to document the details of the incident and try to collect any physical evidence. Then I would report it to my senior."

What would you do if you suspect that a passenger is suspicious or a high risk to passengers?

"I would keep watch before reporting to the senior any abnormal behaviour indicating a suspicious passenger."

What would you do and how would you react in a hijacking?

"I would remain calm, and follow the emergency guidelines and procedures."

How would you act in an emergency such as a crash landing?

"As soon as I get the warning that something is going to happen, I would get a plan together in my mind. I would stay calm and in control and follow the emergency guidelines and procedures."

If you were going to Mars, what three items would you take?

"First, I would take a trained astronaut. Second, sufficient food for the journey and finally, enough fuel for the return trip."

Role-play
SCENARIOS

Role-play scenarios will bear some relation to the demands of the position, even if this is not immediately apparent. The scenarios are used to reveal key competencies required for the position and are likely to include:

Intoxicated passenger	Disorderly behaviour
Terrorist threat	Disruptive child
Toilet smoker	Abusive behaviour
Fearful passenger	Passenger complaint

The assessors don't expect you to know the answer to every possible scenario they introduce. They simply want to see how you react in challenging situations. So when taking part in any role play scenario, use the following guidelines:

- Be proactive and do your best to resolve the situation using your initiative
- Remain calm and composed
- Be direct and assertive
- Immerse yourself into the role
- Take each scenario seriously
- Devise a plan and follow it as much as possible

Here are some pointers to help you deal with some common scenarios:

Complaint

In the case of a passenger complaint, it is important that you listen to their concern without interruption. Ask questions, where appropriate, to clarify their concerns and show empathy towards their situation. If the facts warrant it, apologise for the situation, explain what action you intend to take and thank them for bringing the matter to your attention.

Fearful passenger

If a passenger is fearful of flying, be considerate of their feelings. Use a gentle and calm tone to talk them through the flight and reassure them of any sounds or sensations they may experience. Let the passenger know where you can be found and show them the call bell.

Intoxicated passenger

Offer the passenger a cup of tea or coffee and don't provide any more alcoholic drinks. You could also encourage the passenger to eat some food. Remain calm towards the passenger, but be direct and assertive in your approach. If you feel it appropriate, inform your senior and seek assistance from other crewmembers.

Sell me this pen

The interviewer may ask a question such as this in an attempt to throw you off guard and see how you react to on the spot questions. The question isn't about the product you are being asked to sell, and selling isn't a part of the job. Read between the lines and you will discover that the interviewer will be assessing: How well do you respond to pressure? How quickly can you think on your feet? Do you think before you speak? How well do you research and present information? Do you focus on the positives or negatives?

Before delving in and answering this question, demonstrate your attention to detail by asking for a few moments while you examine the product. During this period, take the opportunity to write with it. Click the pen on and off. Examine the feel of the pen as it touches the paper and look at the flow of ink. Notice everything you can that could be viewed as a benefit. Is the ink vivid? Does it glide smoothly across the paper? Does it feel substantial in your hand? Is is light and easy to hold? Is it disposable and inexpensive to replace?

Once you have a good understanding of the pen, reiterate these positive benefits back to the interviewer.

If the interviewer throws an objection, they are looking to see how you handle adversity. In this instance, remain calm, acknowledge the objection, and restate the benefits as appropriate. Remember, the task is unimportant, but the way you react is vital.

MAKE A SUCCESSFUL CLOSE

Have you stretched the truth today to gain a favourable outcome?

"Absolutely not. I haven't tried to be someone I am not, because I wouldn't want to get the job that way. To do so would be such a short term gain because eventually I would be found out."

How would you respond if we told you that you have been unsuccessful on this occasion?

"Naturally, I will be a disappointed if I do not secure this job with you because it is something I really want, I feel ready for it, and I have had plenty to contribute. However, I am not one to give up quickly. I will think about where I went wrong and how I could have done better, and I would then take steps towards strengthening my candidacy."

What would you say if I said your skills and experience were below the requirements of this job?

"I would ask what particular aspects of my skills and experience you felt were lacking and address each one of those areas with examples of where my skills and experiences do match your requirements. I would expect that after this discussion you would be left in no doubt about my ability to do this job."

Aren't you overqualified for this position?

"I wouldn't say that I am overqualified, but certainly fully qualified. With more than the minimal experience, I offer immediate returns on your investment. Don't you want a winner with the skill sets and attitudes to do just that?"

What question could I ask that would intimidate you?

"I can't think of any question that would intimidate me. This is probably the most intimidating question."

How would you rate me as a recruiter?

"First, I'd give you high marks for your people skills. You helped me feel at ease right away, which made it easier for me to answer the questions. I'd also rate you highly on the creativity of the questions, and their thoroughness. By probing me as carefully as you have, you've given me a better opportunity to secure this position. You've given me a complete picture of what to expect at Fly High Airlines, and it confirms my belief that this is where I want to work."

I'm not sure you are suitable for the position. Convince me.

"I am absolutely suitable. In fact, I am confident that I am perfect for this position.

You are looking for someone who is customer focused. Well, as you can see from my résumé, I have worked in client facing roles for eight years so have had plenty of experience dealing with the various aspects. I also run a successful business that relies on customer satisfaction. The fact that I am still in business, and have a solid and increasing client base, is a clear testament to my abilities.

Furthermore, you need someone who has a calm approach, and retains their composure in the face of adversity. Again, I have demonstrated this capability on several occasions throughout my career.

Beyond this, I have a friendly and optimistic character. I am hard working, I thrive on challenges and will always strive to deliver the highest standard of service to your passengers.

I am confident that my skills, experience and personal qualities will complement your existing team and allow me to make a positive contribution to the airline's ongoing success."

So you do still wish us to consider you for this position?

"Absolutely! Having had this chance to meet you and learn more about the airline and position, I am even more eager than before. I am convinced that this is the opportunity I am seeking, and I know I can make a positive contribution."

Would you take this job if we offered it to you?

"Yes, definitely. I was eager as soon as I saw the job opening on your web site. More than that though, actually meeting potential colleagues and finding out more about the airline and the position has clarified still further what an exciting challenge it would be to work here."

When are you available to start if offered the position?

"I have the energy and enthusiasm to start straight away. All I need is a week's notice and I'm ready."

Do you have any reservations about working here?

"I don't have any reservations at this point. I see this position as a fine opportunity, and the airline as one I would be proud to be an employee of."

Can we contact previous employers for references?

"Yes, absolutely. I'm confident that all my references will be favourable and will confirm what we've discussed here today."

Ask the

RIGHT QUESTIONS

This section of the interview is a real chance for you to shine and set yourself apart from all the other candidates. Therefore, it is a good idea to prepare one or two intelligent questions in advance.

The questions you ask, and how you ask them, say a lot about you, your motives, your depth of knowledge about the airline and the position itself.

Guidelines

The questions you ask should follow these guidelines:

» Don't ask questions that could be easily answered through your own research.

» Ask questions which demonstrate a genuine interest in and knowledge of the airline and the position.

» Demonstrate that you know just that little bit more than is required.

Question About Suitability

Asking recruiters to raise their concerns about your suitability will provide you with an opportunity to follow up and reassure the recruiter.

- » Do you have any reservations about my ability to do this job?
- » What do you foresee as possible obstacles or problems I might have?
- » Is there anything else I need to do to maximise my chances of getting this job?
- » How does my background compare with others you have interviewed?
- » Is there anything else you'd like to know?
- » What do you think are my strongest assets and possible weaknesses?
- » Do you have any concerns that I need to clear up in order to be a considered candidate?

Questions About the Recruiter

Asking recruiters about their views and experience in the job or working with the airline will demonstrate your genuine interest and motives.

- » How did you find the transition in relocating to ...?
- » Why did you choose to work at ... airlines?
- » What is it about this airline that keeps you working here?
- » It sounds as if you really enjoy working here, what have you enjoyed most about working for ... airlines?

General Questions

» How would you describe the company culture?

» I feel my background and experience are a good fit for this position, and I am very interested. What is the next step?

» Yes, when do I start?

No Questions

» I did have plenty of questions, but we've covered them all during our discussions. I was particularly interested in ... but we've dealt with that thoroughly.

» I had many questions, but you've answered them all you have been so helpful. I'm even more excited about this opportunity than when I applied.

Questions to Avoid

You should avoid asking questions such as those following as they will make you appear selfishly motivated.

» How many day's holiday allowances will I receive?

» What is the salary?

» When will I receive a pay increase?

» How many free flights will my family receive?

» Can I request flights to ...?

THE

CONCLUSION

WHAT NEXT?

What happens

NEXT?

Following the final interview, airlines aim to follow up with candidates within two to eight weeks. This is the time that is most difficult, and it is unlikely that you will sleep soundly as you wait of the outome of the interview.

If you are successful, you can expect to receive a job offer from the recruitment department by email, telephone and/or letter within the noted time frame. ,

For those candidates who have been successful, you will be advised of the various pre joining clearance requirements. These may include:

Preemployment medical test
Reference checks
Joining forms

Once the required steps of the process have been completed, the airline will make the necessary arrangements to deliver the employment contract and relevant documentation. You will also be given final clearance to resign from your current employer.

Coping with
SETBACKS

It may seem counter intuitive to provide coping strategies for rejection in an interview guidance book, however, in an industry such as this, where supply exceeds demand, rejection is an unfortunate outcome that some candidates will ultimately face.

So, rather than be crushed by this outcome, I have put together the following tips for coping with, learning from and moving forward following a setback.

Prepare

The popular saying 'Prepare for the worst, but hope for the best' certainly applies in interview scenarios. If you attend the interview with an open mind, your attitude will be more relaxed, you will be better prepared and your coping abilities will be greatly enhanced.

Assess

Faced with rejection, it can be easy to misplace blame on yourself, others or on the general circumstances. But, if you are to learn and grow from your experience, you must be objective and logical in your assessment, rather than making rash and unsubstantiated assumptions.

Firstly, you need to reflect on your own performance to establish any possible areas for improvement. You can then make adjustments as necessary and shift your focus to the next opportunity.

Firstly, you need to reflect on your own performance to establish any possible areas for improvement. In this assessment, you could ask:

Did I dress appropriately?
How did I sound?
Did I arrive on time?
Did I remember to smile?
Did I appear confident and relaxed?
Could my answers have been improved?
Did I maintain appropriate eye contact?
Did I establish rapport with the recruiter?

If this assessment identifies any weaknesses, you can make adjustments as necessary and shift your focus to the next opportunity.

Accept

Sometimes factors exist that are beyond your control and the unfortunate outcome may not have been directly influenced by your performance at all. In this instance, all you can do is accept the outcome and shift your focus to the next opportunity.

Be positive

Whatever the reason for rejection, it is important to treat each setback as a learning experience. So, don't become obsessive or overly critical, keep an open mind and be open to change if necessary. By handling the setback in this way, you will move forward and succeed much more quickly.

I would love

TO HEAR FROM YOU

If you have enjoyed reading this guide and have found it useful, I would love to hear from you, so please consider leaving your feedback.

www.CabinCrew.Guide

Where dreams are made

Facebook

CPSIA information can be obtained
at www.ICGtesting.com
Printed in the USA
BVHW011748211118
533744BV00010B/114/P